AS ONE WITH AUTHORITY

Also by Jackson W. Carroll
Carriers of Faith:
Lessons from Congregational Studies
(Edited with Carl S. Dudley
and James P. Wind)

AS ONE WITH AUTHORITY

Reflective Leadership in Ministry

Jackson W. Carroll

Westminster/John Knox Press
Louisville, Kentucky

Design by Ken Taylor

First edition

Published by Westminster/John Knox Press
Louisville, Kentucky

PRINTED IN THE UNITED STATES OF AMERICA
9 8 7 6 5 4 3 2 1

Library of Congress Cataloging-in-Publication Data

Carroll, Jackson W.
    As one with authority : reflective leadership in ministry / Jackson W. Carroll. — 1st ed.
        p.   cm.
    Includes bibliographical references.
    ISBN 0-664-25168-4

    1. Clergy—Office.   2. Authority (Religion)   I. Title.
262'.1—dc20   91-15205

CONTENTS

84510

PREFACE

This book is an effort to recover a valid meaning of authority in an age that, for a variety of reasons, has rejected old hierarchical notions of authority. It proposes a way of reconceiving and exercising authority for ministry that takes seriously the ministry that the whole people of God share. I call this perspective *reflective leadership*, and I attempt to indicate what this kind of leadership looks like in practice. In the book, I build on and extend considerably some ideas that I put forward in an earlier work, *Ministry as Reflective Practice* (Carroll 1986).

I recognize, of course, that for some clergy and laity authority does not pose a problem. Fundamentalist Christians settle authority issues with reference to an infallible scripture; Catholic traditionalists continue to look to an infallible teaching office; the authority of clergy in many African-American churches has been unusually strong and often unquestioned. For these groups a book such as this, which proposes a way of reconceiving authority, may be addressing questions that they are not asking. For many others, however, authority issues are real and their consequences often painful. It is for them especially that I intend the book. I hope, however, that all clergy will find it helpful in thinking about their exercise of authority and leadership in the church.

In the book, I refer to clergy variously as ordained ministers, pastors, and priests. While I have tried to be sensitive to differences in these titles where appropriate, I have often used them interchangeably. I have also tried to use the unmodified term "ministry" to refer both to laity and clergy. I realize that my use of "ordained minister" may create a problem for some in the Reformed tradition who also ordain laity as ruling elders. Also, though I am committed to the use of inclusive language, this has not always been possible in citations where the author used gender-specific language.

My perspective on authority draws heavily on my own discipline of sociology. In last analysis, however, I have been rather eclectic. I have found much help from works of historians, biblical scholars, and theologians. Deserving special mention are practicing pastors, especially those with whom I have worked closely in Hartford Seminary's doctor of ministry program. They have shared their wisdom with me in many ways. Insights from a number of them are included in this book, as are also those from a group of clergy in the Hartford area who allowed me to sit with them over a number of weeks as they discussed their ministry practice. The latter group includes the Revs. William Eakins, Richard Griffis, James Kidd, Archie McCree, and Paul Santmire.

I also am grateful to others who have patiently listened to—in some cases endured would be more accurate—my ideas about ministry practice and have shared their criticisms and insights with me. My colleagues at Hartford Seminary have been important partners with me in exploring the meanings of reflective practice. I am particularly grateful to Clifford Green, who gave critical feedback on several chapters. Gary Bouma also read and commented on the manuscript. The Project Team for

Congregational Studies (Nancy Ammerman, Rebecca Chopp, Carl Dudley, Ardith Hayes, William Holway, William McKinney, and Barbara Wheeler) spent a day discussing an earlier version of the manuscript and giving constructive feedback. Early in my work, I benefited from conversations with Donald Schön, whose ideas, as will be evident, are central to my argument. I am also appreciative of the helpful and careful editorial suggestions made by Alexa Smith, Danielle Alexander, and Dawn Ripley of Westminster/John Knox Press.

I owe a special debt of gratitude to the Lilly Endowment, and to Robert Wood Lynn, formerly Senior Vice President of the Endowment and now retired. A grant from the Endowment supported a part of my research. Equally important was Bob Lynn's generous gift of his wisdom and encouragement. Additionally, a Basic Issues Grant from the Association of Theological Schools made possible earlier research that was important to parts of this book.

I dedicate the book to my wife, Anne Ewing Carroll. Her patience, prodding, nurture, and support have been crucial. I have also learned a great deal from the ways that she has exercised reflective leadership in her ministry as a layperson.

PLAN OF THE BOOK

In the first chapter, I indicate why I believe clergy face a crisis of authority. Several vignettes provide insights into ways in which clergy and congregations experience the crisis. I also discuss factors which have contributed to the authority crisis.

In chapter 2, I try to "unpack" the meaning of authority in relation to clergy. First, I ask what authority for ministry involves, especially for ordained ministry. From what does ministry derive its authority? Following a discussion of the ultimate basis of authority in the church, I focus especially on two penultimate bases of clergy authority: clergy as representatives of the sacred and the clergyperson's specialized knowledge or expertise.

Chapter 3 continues the discussion of authority, addressing what I call the "relational dimension" of authority: the relationship between clergy and laity and the degree to which each shares authority for ministry. I use several examples from the history of the church to point out how authority relationships have varied under changing social and cultural circumstances.

With these two chapters as a general perspective on clergy authority, I turn to the task of reconceiving clergy authority in light of the issues that confront the church and its ministry today. This necessitates spelling out some assumptions that I make about the church and its ministry, which I do in chapter 4. Chapter 5 builds on these assumptions. From a perspective of shared ministry, I indicate what I believe to be the distinctive tasks of leadership that the church needs, especially from its clergy. My purpose is to provide a phenomenology of ministry practice as a basis for reconceiving the exercise of clergy authority.

What does it to mean to exercise authority from within the framework of a shared ministry of clergy and laity? Answering this question involves a rethinking of the meaning of both expertise and representing the sacred, which I attempt in the final three chapters. I do so under the rubric of "reflective leadership," building in part on the work of Schön (1983, 1987), who has proposed a new paradigm for professional practice generally. Chapter 6 explores the dynamics of reflective leadership, using case material from clergy practice. In chapter 7, I focus on the structure of reflective leadership, considering the various ingredients that come to bear in one's practice of ministry leadership. Finally, in chapter 8, I ask what it means today to represent the sacred and how this relates to the expertise that reflective leadership requires.

In many respects, this book itself is an example of

reflective practice, as perhaps the reader will understand more fully at the end. It grows out of a vision of ministry that I have tried to articulate in some detail. Its multi-disciplinary perspective, drawing on a variety of resources, is also a clue to its character as reflective practice. And, it has gone through several stages of framing and reframing the issues as I have reflected on ministry practice and listened to "talkback" from the situation, especially from clergy and colleagues.

AS ONE WITH AUTHORITY

1

As One Without Authority?

"And when Jesus finished these sayings, the crowds were astonished at his teaching, for he taught them as one who had authority, and not as their scribes."

—Matthew 7:28–29

QUESTION AUTHORITY
—popular bumper sticker

The bumper sticker "QUESTION AUTHORITY" became popular as a reflection of the intense questioning of all forms of authority by the late 1960s counterculture. It was an exhortation, not a call to self-doubt. Yet that is what it has come to be for many ordained ministers who, for a host of reasons, are unsure of their authority as leaders of the church. In contrast to the way that the crowds experienced Jesus, many clergy experience themselves "as one[s] *without* authority," the title of a helpful book on preaching (Craddock 1979, emphasis supplied). This is far from the "awesome powers" that the early Puritan preachers exercised in their congregations and New England towns. As Harry Stout has written in his

13

history of preaching and religious culture in colonial New England, "Their sermons were the only voice of authority that congregations were pledged to obey unconditionally" (1986, 19).

Authority is the right to exercise leadership in a particular group or institution based upon a combination of qualities, characteristics, or expertise that the leader has or that followers believe their leader has. To exercise authority involves influencing, directing, coordinating, or otherwise guiding the thought and behavior of persons and groups in ways that they consider legitimate. Within the Christian tradition, clergy have authority through ordination to proclaim the Word of God, to administer the sacraments, to exercise pastoral care and oversight, and to equip the laity for ministry. Denominations use different rubrics for ordination and interpret it differently, but these are the charter functions for which most churches grant authority to clergy in their ordination. In the exercise of these functions, many clergy come to "question authority"—their own!

Let me be autobiographical. When a Methodist bishop laid his hands on my head in an ordination service, speaking for the church he authorized me to fulfill those charter functions of ministry. As a parish and campus minister for nine years, I attempted to do so as faithfully and effectively as I could. Along the way, I encountered more or less routine challenges to my authority to lead: mild disagreements over procedures, reminders that my predecessors had done things differently, occasional questioning of sermon content or (especially) hymn selection, and initial opposition to building a new educational wing to the church.

The first and major challenge to my authority came over racial justice issues. Members questioned and sharply criticized both my preaching and public activities. I survived these challenges primarily because of the support of my district superintendent and the positive relationships I had developed with parishioners over the years. They had come to trust me and care for me even when they sharply disagreed with my sermons and activities. Still, I discovered that the bloom was off the roses: My authority to preach, teach, and lead had been sorely tested.

A second major challenge to my authority during those years was more an internal one, though triggered by the university context in which I ministered. As a campus minister, I struggled to preach and teach the gospel in a setting whose epistemological assumptions radically challenged the ultimate basis of my authority: God and God's action in history, to which I was called to bear witness. I became acutely aware of the gulf that exists between certainty of belief in a transcendent God who acts in history and a perspective that rules out all knowledge that one cannot verify empirically. Granted, many in the university shared my unease; nevertheless, for me it was an acute challenge to my authority for ministry with which I had to come to terms. I became existentially aware of the truth of Paul's words that "now we see in a mirror dimly" (1 Cor. 13:12).

Also during these nine years, I was tested by the complex issues facing our society: racism, nuclear armaments and world peace, technological changes, the challenges of abundance and poverty. I was also acutely conscious of the difficulty of addressing these issues as a Christian in ways that might make a real difference. Even if my calling and ordination gave me authority to wrestle with such issues, what impact could I or the church have?

How much those experiences led me away from the parish to exercise my ministry in a teaching role as a sociologist in a theological seminary, I cannot say. I do know, however, that they did not diminish my interest in ordained ministry nor my commitment to the ministry of God's people. In particular, these experiences have made me acutely sensitive to authority issues faced by clergy whom I have taught, observed, and interacted with in congregational and other settings. I believe that questioning one's authority to lead in ministry has not diminished; if anything, it has increased. Consider the following vignettes, which reflect typical—and real—experiences of clergy:

• A clergywoman finds herself running from meeting to meeting, appointment to appointment, seven days a week. In a rare moment of self-reflection, she asks herself, near exhaustion, "What is it all for? Does it add up to anything important?"

• A pastor in a church with a congregational polity wants his congregation to participate in an ecumenical program to address racism in the community. Sadly, however, he confesses that he must decline because it would risk alienating too many members. He adds sardonically, "It's a matter of tiptoeing through the tithers."

• A denomination that has lost members annually over a twenty-year period is almost paranoic over the loss. Its leaders have become increasingly shrill in their calls for reversing the trends. Many local church clergy and lay leaders in the denomination share the crisis mentality. They join the denomination's leaders in grasping at every straw of program or technique that promises growth, rarely asking "Why?" or "For what purpose?"

• A young pastor, four years out of seminary, is confronted with a series of difficult pastoral problems, including a major conflict that has erupted in his parish council. He discovers that he is ill-prepared to deal with the problems, at a loss to apply the theory learned in seminary to these and other parish situations. He becomes disillusioned and angry at the failure of his seminary education.

• A Catholic priest, now well along in years, expresses frustration and is sometimes bitter over the growth of parishioner resistance to a leadership style that served him well for so long. For years, laity allowed him—no, expected him—to call the shots in parish affairs. Why now do they so often resist his decisions, insisting on having a voice in setting directions for the parish? His counterpart in a black Protestant congregation expresses a similar frustration as once pliant laity ask for a share in decision making.

• A new seminary graduate is imbued with an egalitarian theology of a shared ministry of clergy and laity. It surprises, frustrates, disappoints, even embitters him when he discovers that laity expect him to lead, to be directive. They treat him as an expert; he wants to be an enabler.

• A pastor of a growing congregation finds considerable affirmation and success through a ministry of one-to-one counseling, sermons that center on individual fulfillment, and what he sometimes calls a "supermarket" of programs. "I know where my members itch, and I've learned how to scratch that itch," he says somewhat jokingly to a group of clergy colleagues as they discuss their understanding of ministry.

• A pastor prides herself on a well-run church. She keeps herself busy with administrative duties, attends meetings faithfully, and visits parishioners in need. The worship services that she leads are well-planned and carried out. Why, then, do some of her lay members complain that something is missing from the church? They sense a lack of spiritual depth. Some say, "She knows about God, but she doesn't seem to know God personally."

• A college senior who has an outstanding record as a student and campus leader feels called to the ordained ministry. As she wrestles with the decision, she wonders whether a congregation is the most effective setting in which to exercise her gifts of leadership. "Isn't the church marginal to where important decisions are made in our society?" she muses. "Can't I make a more important contribution elsewhere?" She chooses to go to law school instead.

Despite their diversity, and while risking caricature, each of these vignettes reflects experiences of real-life clergy. Moreover, whether it is immediately apparent or not, each reflects issues of authority and leadership: frantic busyness that seems to go nowhere; fear of alienating influential members; grasping at means without considering ends; inability to make sense of the complex "messes" one finds in many parishes; resistance to authoritarian leadership, on the one hand, and demands for expertise on the other; uncritically accommodating the Christian gospel to the culture; managing well but lacking religious authenticity; wondering whether being an ordained minister is the best way to make a difference. The list could be expanded, but it is unnecessary to do so.

The point is that many clergy—and lay leaders as well—have serious questions about their authority to lead and have difficulty knowing how to do so. Further, such issues as low morale, debilitating stress, burnout, and perhaps even some of the moral failures of clergy that have garnered so much media attention in recent years are also related to this questioning of authority. They are often triggered by similar dilemmas and situations as those described in the vignettes.

The opportunity that this crisis presents is that of rethinking issues of authority for ministry and discovering ways of exercising it that are faithful to the gospel and appropriate to the church's life and ministry in the late twentieth century. That is my purpose in this book: to provide a perspective on authority and how it can be exercised that will help clergy who experience the frustrations over authority that the vignettes highlight.

To what extent are questions of authority and leadership new? Aren't the examples sketched in the vignettes of long standing? The answer in one sense is yes. Questions of clergy authority have been with the church since its beginning. Each generation of the church has confronted its own version of these issues. While there is continuity between present and past ways of framing the issues, each generation has had to face challenges and opportunities peculiar to its own time. "New occasions teach new duties," as the old hymn expresses it. Thus, the present provides its own special challenge for understanding and exercising authority to lead the church in ministry.

FACTORS AFFECTING
CLERGY AUTHORITY AND LEADERSHIP

What has made it difficult for many clergy to lead with authority at the present time? It would be tempting to "blame the victim" and imply that the problem lies within clergy themselves. Certainly clergy are not blameless, but many of the difficulties clergy face over authority originate in broad social and cultural changes that have been occurring over many years that have affected the churches and consequently clergy as well. While these complex changes will not be examined in any detail, four factors are of particular importance: the questioning of fundamental assumptions about God, the marginalization of the church itself, dependence upon voluntarism in the work of the church, and, finally, clergy emphasis on shared ministry with laity.

A CRISIS OF BELIEF

The first is the perception of the historicity or relativity of our knowledge and beliefs characteristic of what some call a postmodern age. Our most fundamental assumptions about God and God's purposes for human life are called into question. This was what challenged me as a campus minister, and I believe that I am not unique in this experience.

In Marc Connelly's play *Green Pastures*, the angel Gabriel is sent to survey the world scene and reports back that "everything nailed down is coming loose!" Both the achievements of the sciences and the pluralism of modern life have made us excruciatingly aware of the accuracy of Gabriel's observation. Both science and pluralism make it increasingly difficult for us to speak confidently of "timeless truths" or "eternal certainties" that we can express in precise doctrinal formulations or unchanging moral principles. Instead, we speak of our faith in terms of myths, metaphors, and symbols. Of course, many fundamentalist Christians continue to speak of their faith with great certainty, and if Dean Kelley (1972) is correct, this is one of the secrets of conservative church growth in recent years. Yet even many conservative Christians find it difficult to avoid the challenges of modernity and attempt to smooth over and modify the content and style of their beliefs to make them more acceptable to contemporary men and women.[1] Whether we are conservative or liberal, our life experiences regularly remind us that life is a multi-possibility affair, and those multiple possibilities include radically different ways of construing and living it, including holding differing views of God and God's purposes for human life, or no belief in God at all.

As long as we lived in a culture that generally shared the assumptions of a Christian perspective, or at least a Judeo-Christian perspective, we could ignore the challenge of other faiths. Even when there were competing ways of understanding life, we were able to compartmentalize our lives so that the presuppositions and claims made upon us—for example, in business or politics—were segregated from claims made upon us in our religious lives. While it is still possible for us to live in this fragmented, segmented way, doing so requires an increasing amount of legerdemain and self-deception implied in Jean-Paul Sartre's (1956) pregnant concept of "bad faith," through which one hides the truth from one's self. Communications technology, the ease of travel, residential mobility, and the growth of a highly multicultural society make it difficult to take much for granted or to segment our lives so neatly.

Let me refer to another biographical incident that may seem to some to reflect a long-past era. I grew up in the American South during the 1930s and '40s. Although I was aware that others in and outside the region challenged the truth of the Southern Way of Life (a euphemism for *de jure* segregation), I generally accepted it as a taken-for-granted fact of life. My conversion—(that's the only way to describe it)—came when, at age fifteen, I took my first trip outside the South to attend a national church youth conference that was racially integrated. When I returned and was asked to report on the conference to the congregation during the morning worship, I was faced with a quandary: Dare I speak of my conversion on matters of race and risk, declaring my newfound conviction that the god of racism is dead, or should I gloss over that part of the experience and confine my report to "safe" matters? With fear and trembling I took the former course, which was generally written off as youthful, misguided idealism, probably with a mental note to be careful in the future about letting the youth participate in such subversive activities.

Today, it is more difficult to write off such experiences, as my fellow church members did. One travels to other cultures with different religious traditions and experiences what it is like to be in the minority. Closer to home, one's son or daughter becomes a Moonie or a Hare Krishna. One's next door neighbor is a Muslim or a Buddhist. One's best friend is a practicing New Age spiritualist. One is also faced with the incredible complexity of moral issues in business, medicine, international affairs, or one's personal life. And regularly, one is challenged by African-American, feminist, or third-world critiques of one's taken-for-granted beliefs and assumptions. Such events and experiences make it extremely difficult to ignore beliefs that are in radical opposition to one's own or to assert with conviction one's belief in absolute, eternal truths and moral principles.

The dilemma I faced as a young teenager in questioning the Southern Way of Life seems mild in comparison to the challenge that we face some forty years later. It is a challenge that goes to the heart of our beliefs about God and God's purposes, and not only clergy but laity face it as well. Many laity no longer hold to the faith as if it were a whole cloth that can be accepted in its entirety. Instead, they pick and choose among fragments of the tradition, even as consumers pick and choose among different products. Postmodern philosophers (e.g., Lyotard 1984) have called this "the end of the great narratives." Canadian sociologist Reginald Bibbey (1987, 83) puts it more vividly: "The gods of old have been neither abandoned nor replaced. Rather, they have been broken into pieces and offered to religious consumers in piecemeal form."

How are clergy to speak with authority in such an ethos, much less lead? Is it even possible to speak with authority at all? There is an old baseball story about three umpires. When asked how they made their calls of balls and strikes, the first answered, "I call them as they are." The second replied, "I call them as I see them." Whereupon the third said, "They ain't nothing until I call them." While there is a profound epistemological debate summarized in the story (to which I return in a later chapter), I simply note here that many clergy and laity would like to be able to "call them as they are," based on some absolute authority of an infallible scripture or ecclesiastical institution. Since that is no longer possible for many of us, we are left with either of the latter two options, both of which involve acknowledging the radically perspectival character of our efforts to speak a word from the Lord in either a tentative or a boldly confessional stance. Either way involves risk and vulnerability that are not easy to endure, as Fred Craddock recognizes in this description of the dilemma of the preacher:

> Does the fact that [the preacher's] own faith is in process, always becoming but never fully and finally arrived, disqualify him from the pulpit? Not really feeling he is a member of the congregation he serves, he is hesitant to let it be known when his own faith is crippled for fear of causing the whole congregation to limp. It is this painful conflict between the traditional expectation of him and honesty with himself, a conflict so dramatically heightened in our time, that gives the minister pause and often frightens him from the pulpit (1971, 14).

FROM THE CENTER TO THE PERIPHERY

Historicity and relativity affect clergy authority primarily at the cultural level, at the level of consciousness and thought. A second factor that contributes to the crisis of authority is primarily institutional or structural in character. It involves a shift in the social location of the church from the center to the periphery.

When the young college student described earlier in one of the vignettes decided against ordained ministry and opted for law school, she gave as her reason a perception that is now widespread, especially among mainline (or mainstream) Protestants[2], namely, that the church today is marginal in our society and that the clergy role is thereby diminished. Whether this perception is true or not, it has important consequences for ordained ministers' feelings about their authority and exercise of leadership.

The perception is based on assumptions about the broad process of secularization whereby the church has moved from being a central institution, with considerable authority to prescribe normative expectations for other social institutions, to a place on the periphery. Most of us no longer view major social institutions as having a religious basis or as expressions of divinely established "orders of creation," as they were in the *societas christiana* that came to its fullest fruition in the Middle Ages. Instead, over the years such institutions—political, economic, military, educational, leisure, and, to a lesser degree, familial—have become autonomous, free from the authority of the church. They have their own proximate ends—for example, maximizing profit, providing political stability, teaching individuals the knowledge and skills necessary to function efficiently in other institutional contexts, providing a context for meeting expressive needs—that have little, if any, reference to an overarching ultimate or sacred purpose, except perhaps at certain ceremonial occasions such as political rallies, Memorial Day, or the Fourth of July. Further, leaders in these institutions search for functionally rational means for the achievement of these proximate ends through modern science and technology. Jacques Ellul (1964) has called this the triumph of "technique"—the search for the "one best way."

The church is now one functionally specific organization among several, with no authority (legitimacy) to prescribe or dictate appropriate behavior in other sectors of society. At best, church leaders can attempt to influence decisions and actions more indirectly by morally persuasive analysis and interpretation. A major exception is the family, one institution where churches still have an important, though unofficial, role as shaper of values and norms. This too is changing as families are increasingly shaped by other social forces, including changing gender roles and the large-scale entry of women into the work force. To use the categories of sociologist Thomas Luckmann (1967), there is now a *public* sphere, dominated by major economic and political institutions, and a *private* sphere, consisting of the family, a variety of voluntary associations, and various forms of leisure activities through which individuals pursue self-fulfillment. For the most part the church, too, is part of this private sphere, at the margins rather than the center of society.

Clergy are caught in this movement of the church from the center to the margins of society. Although the public still holds clergy in high esteem, as numerous opinion polls show, there is a widespread belief that the clergy's primary role is to help individuals deal with the issues of their private lives. Few ordained ministers have not been told, "Stick to the gospel! Leave politics alone!" Public issues, if not out of bounds, are often viewed as secondary to the church's primary task.

Even when this is not the case, the issues of members' public lives—issues in their worlds of work, for example—have become increasingly distant and distinct from their private experiences and often quite complex and technical, and the same is true for various public issues. Clergy who try to help members think through the ethical issues raised in their work settings or address issues of public policy often find themselves at a disadvantage. As sociologist Ivan Vallier (1968, 453) has commented:

> The clergyman lacks a technical body of knowledge which can be applied to the solution of empirical problems. . . . For the most part his knowledge is normative and closed, rather than scientific and open. He interprets while his colleagues in the secular professions prescribe; he tries to give meaning to the event, since he cannot control it.

As I will note in a subsequent chapter, this by no means need be interpreted negatively. The effort by clergy to understand issues of the public sector and to present morally persuasive interpretations of such issues from a faith perspective constitutes an important role. The difficulty of doing so, however, contributes further to the sense that many clergy have of marginality and con-

sequent doubts about their authority and capacity to
lead.

VOLUNTARISM

A third factor contributing to the clergy's uncertainty about their authority is the voluntary character of
American religious life. Voluntarism is the peculiarly
American way of responding to the disestablishment of
religion that I described in the preceding paragraphs. As
is well known, American churches and synagogues are
voluntary associations of persons, typically like-minded,
who freely choose to come together to give expression to
their religious convictions and work for common purposes. As voluntary associations, they depend on the
voluntary participation and support of their members.
No religious group can claim special legal prerogatives or
support not enjoyed by all others. This situation has
given rise to American denominationalism and to the religiously pluralistic system of which it is a part.

Religious voluntarism has had a major impact on
many aspects of American life, including clergy authority. The latter has been discussed in some detail by Sidney Mead (1956) and James Gustafson (1963). Mead
notes that in the early days of the nation the voluntary
principle made localism and congregationalism especially
strong, shearing clergy of much of the authority of office
that a religious establishment would have provided. Voluntarism, with its purposive character, also increased ordained ministers' need to rely on persuasion and politics,
demonstrations of effectiveness (especially in saving
souls), and personal piety as principal bases of their authority. Moreover, the localistic and congregationalist aspects of voluntarism meant that clergy had to learn to
live face-to-face with laity, with no denominational judi-
catories—at least in the early days—to provide a buffer
or court of appeal. Mead (p. 217) quotes French philosophe Michel-Guillaume-Jean de Crèvecoeur who, in *Let-*

ters From an American Farmer, "conceives no other idea of a clergyman than that of a hired man; if he does his work he will pay him the stipulated sum; if not he will dismiss him, and do without his sermons, and let his church be shut up for years."

It was a combination of responses to various aspects of this voluntary approach to religion, especially its laicism and its emphasis on effectiveness, that were major contributors to the self-conscious professionalization of the ordained ministry in the mid-nineteenth century. Participating in what was a more general move toward professionalizing occupations during this time, clergy sought to gain more control over their own circumstances than voluntarism allowed, because of its localism, congregationalism, and potential for laicism. This was also accompanied by a move to make theological education more practical, more responsive to the need for clergy who could function effectively in leading congregations.

Gustafson extends Mead's historical analysis to the more recent period. He notes in particular the way that voluntarism and its accompanying denominationalism create competition among clergy to win the support of current and prospective members. "The laity have a buyer's market in religion, and the clergy find those ways which will gain for their church a fair share of the market" (Gustafson 1963, 733). Since Gustafson wrote, the church growth movement has burst on the American religious scene offering clergy pragmatic ways of reaching the buyer's market, often with little apparent theological rationale other than the stemming of membership decline or growth for the institution's sake. Like Mead, Gustafson emphasizes the importance of voluntarism for creating an instrumental or functional approach to ministry in order to win and maintain the favor of laity:

> The praise of God for his goodness and power does not legitimate a clergyman in the United States. He is expected to be engaged in practical activities that

affect the lives of the people in his community or congregation. Thus he becomes the psychotherapist, the family counselor, the director of recreation for adolescents, the administrator of multiple organizations in a local congregation (p. 732).

Voluntarism and the importance of lay support also leads clergy to try to extend the relevance of religion to the secular activities that dominate the life of their lay members. As Gustafson says, "If the traditional functions of the clergy make them appear anachronistic, they are prepared to adapt themselves so that they remain in touch with the laity and with the main currents of cultural life" (p. 733).

As Gustafson recognizes, all of this takes its toll on the clergy. They become so busy in so many activities that it is easy to lose sight of the locus of their responsibility. They are responsible not just to laity, not just to their denomination, but to God. And so pastors sometimes find themselves, as in the vignettes that I cited earlier, feeling tempted to try to "scratch every itch" of their lay members to keep their favor, finding it necessary to "tiptoe through the tithers" to avoid giving offense, being technically proficient in managing a well-run church without any overarching vision of its purpose, and feeling that they have lost sight of their calling in the midst of frantic business.

Voluntarism, as Mead and Gustafson make clear, has been with us in the American churches almost from the beginning. It is both an organizational principle and a set of values. Is there anything new about the present situation that exacerbates the authority and leadership issues? I think so, and I believe that it is to be found in an intensification of voluntaristic values of which members of the post–World War II baby boom generation are primary carriers.

Several analysts have described the new voluntaristic values. Pollster Daniel Yankelovich (1981) refers to them as an ethic of self-fulfillment in contrast to an older, Puritan-influenced ethic of self-denial, and he estimates that as much as 80 percent of the American population is caught up in this quest for fulfillment. The most intense seekers, however, are in the under-35 generation. In their book *Habits of the Heart*, Robert Bellah and his associates (1985) further describe this new culture in terms of two forms of individualism, utilitarian and expressive, that have long roots in American culture (especially the utilitarian version). The utilitarian version reigns in the public world, the world of economics and occupational life; the expressive version, which has become increasingly strong in recent years, dominates our private lives. Together they constitute a culture whose "center is the autonomous individual, presumed able to choose the roles he will play and the commitments he will make, not on the basis of higher truths but according to the criterion of life-effectiveness as the individual judges it" (p. 47). The authors continue:

> In its own understanding, the expressive aspect of our culture exists for the liberation and fulfillment of the individual. Its genius is that it enables the individual to think of commitments—from marriage and work to political and religious involvement—as enhancements of the sense of individual well-being rather than as moral imperatives (p. 47).

Echoing similar themes in their analysis of mainline American religion, Wade Clark Roof and William McKinney use the term "new voluntarism" to describe this emerging individualistic culture and lifestyle:

> Today choice means more than simply having an option among religious alternatives; it involves religion as an option itself and opportunity to draw selectively off a variety of traditions in the pursuit of the self. Radically individualistic religion presumes an autonomous believer, one who is on a spiritual

> journey, on his or her own quest. . . . Questions of
> authority, discipline, practice, and common life of-
> ten seem foreign, or at least secondary. Foremost is
> the individual's choice of whether to pursue a 'reli-
> gious matter'; then comes whatever commitments of
> a personal or communal sort, if any, a person may
> choose to make (1987, 40).

The authors conclude that the consequences of these
themes are especially palpable "in the decline of religious
authority and in weakened attachments to organized religion. . . . Traditional channels of authority and respect
for the same—from papal 'infallibility' and biblical 'iner-
rancy' to the spiritual role of the local minister, priest, or
rabbi—have been eroding for some time, but vocal and
outright questioning of these structures increased dra-
matically in the 1960s" (pp. 50–51). In such an ethos
where all authority is questioned, it is little wonder that
clergy question their authority.

EGALITARIANISM AND SHARED MINISTRY

Both in their earlier and more recent expressions,
individualistic, voluntaristic values in American religion
and the broader culture have gone hand in hand with an
egalitarian emphasis, a fourth factor that affects our understanding of clergy authority and its exercise. Hierar-
chies of any kind have been profoundly suspect. With
each individual responsible for his or her own salvation
(now more likely to be defined as self-realization), no one
has any special "pipeline" to God's grace—not priests,
or preachers, or clergy organized into professional
associations.

Egalitarianism finds theological warrant in the doctrine of the priesthood of all believers and the understanding that ministry belongs to the whole people of
God. This means the church's ministry is the calling of all
Christians and not the exclusive preserve of clergy. Dur-

ing the church's long history, there have been pendulum swings between an emphasis on the ministry of all Christians and one where ministry is identified with the clergy role. American religious life has leaned in the former direction. At its best, shared ministry has meant a functional differentiation of clergy and lay roles, each with complementary tasks and with various ways of maintaining some balance of power. Currently, the emphasis on shared ministry is quite strong, not only among Protestants but also for Catholics under the impetus of the Second Vatican Council's teaching that ministry is the responsibility of the whole people of God. Feminist perspectives on ministry, with an emphasis on partnership and mutuality in ministry, have also played an important role in raising the issue. Feminists have resisted structures of authority based on hierarchy and domination.[3]

The emphasis on shared ministry is basic to the perspective of this book. Furthermore, it has helpfully and justifiably called into question the kind of authoritarianism associated with an autocratic style of ministry that keeps laity dependent. Many clergy, like the priest and his counterpart in the African-American congregation in one of vignettes, have had to make painful but necessary adjustments to demands by laity for a greater share in the church's ministry. When they have not done so, they have often faced angry laity and serious conflict, as in a recent case in Connecticut where Catholic parishioners demanded the removal of an autocratic pastor who refused to share the ministry with them.

A caution is in order, however. Shared ministry, ascribed to uncritically without understanding the different but complementary callings of clergy and laity to ministry, can lead to considerable confusion about authority for ministry for clergy and laity alike. For some laity, the confusion has led to the belief that if one is really serious about ministry, he or she needs to attend seminary and become ordained. Shared ministry, in this view, involves every Christian in doing what clergy have

traditionally done. The growing number of older, sec-
ond-career entrants into the ordained ministry may, in
part, reflect this assumption.

The confusion about shared ministry takes a somewhat different tack for clergy. It has led some clergy to
wonder whether there is any distinctive expertise that
they need in order to function in a shared ministry with
laity. Avery Dulles believes that, among Catholics, the
revolt against a traditional sacral conception of ministry
in favor of a shared ministry perspective "is one of the
sources of the present vocations crisis in the Church"
(1978, 174). Others, who work hard at sharing ministry
and think of their role as one who enables, are frustrated
when some laity continue to look to them as experts, as
the young minister described in one of the cases. David
Schuller and his associates, in a major survey of clergy
and laity in the United States and Canada, found that "in
spite of accent within recent years on the work of 'the
whole people of God,' many in the congregation still
view themselves primarily as spectators rather than ones
mutually called to share a ministry with others" (1975,
73). Sociologist Sherryl Kleinman (1984) discovered that
students in a mainline Protestant seminary, who had
adopted a strongly egalitarian approach to ministry, were
surprised and disappointed in their field work and student pastorate experiences when they encountered laity
who treated them as authorities. They understood their
distinctive calling primarily in terms of being "authentic
persons," not experts or authorities who knew more
about some things than laity. Laity, however, looked for
more than this from their pastors. Kleinman interprets
the students' attitudes about the authority and role of
ordained ministers as a move to deprofessionalize the
clergy role, especially to give up a claim to authority
based on special knowledge and expertise. From my perspective, deprofessionalization is a major mistake when
clergy or laity interpret it in such a way as to downplay
the need for expertise and critical thinking in the life of

the church. While clergy have no monopoly on these resources, surely laity have a right to expect clergy to bring to their ministry the specialized knowledge and expertise that their education should have provided—or, in other words, to exercise their authority. As I indicated, I strongly support shared ministry by clergy and laity, but the exercise of clergy authority need not prevent such sharing from occurring. This, however, is to get ahead of the story.

The point for now is that an emphasis on egalitarianism and shared ministry is yet another contributor to the current confusion about authority and leadership in the church. It is an important emphasis, but it joins the perception of the historicity of fundamental beliefs, the changed social location of religion, and voluntarism in leading clergy to question their authority for leadership in the church's ministry.

There is little likelihood that any of us will recover the authoritative status that clergy held in colonial New England—nor would most of us want to do so. The hope here is, nevertheless, that clergy who face issues that cause them to question their authority will find here new bases for claiming their authority and for exercising it as reflective leaders.

2

AUTHORITY IS NOT A FOUR-LETTER WORD

The churches are testaments in stone to an order, security, and timelessness which never will be, either in politics or intimate life. Is it just illusion which compels us to keep building?
—Richard Sennett

Sennett's description of churches reflects the situation that I described in the preceding chapter: What once seemed to be citadels of order, security, and timelessness—and thus a firm foundation for the authority of clergy who lead them—have, for many people, lost their aura of invincibility and absoluteness. Sennett's observation recalls a similar one by the German poet Heinrich Heine, who stood with a friend before the cathedral of Amiens in France.

"Tell me, Heinrich," said his friend, "why can't people build piles like this any more?"

To which Heine replied: "My dear friend, in those days, people had convictions. We moderns have opinions. And it takes more than opinions to build a Gothic cathedral."[1]

What are the consequences for authority? Is it, as Sennett asks, "just illusion which compels us to keep building"—not only churches but other communities and institutions that provide order, security, and meaning? Sennett's answer is no, and I agree. Even if we can no longer sustain many of the convictions that inspired the cathedrals—even if many of us can no longer believe in an infallible church, inerrant scriptures, or the possibility of finding absolute truth that is untouched by our historicity—I believe that our need for authority and authorities is not illusory or diminished. We may question authority, as the bumper sticker admonishes us to do; we may fear authority for its capacity to become authoritarian and oppressive; but we cannot live together for long in any human community without submitting ourselves to the authority of the community's deepest values and norms and to the leadership of those charged with their articulation, interpretation, and realization. No community can function without some form of leadership that enables the community to survive and achieve its goals. Authority is no enemy of community, as we sometimes suppose. Rather, its enemies are tyranny, which coerces obedience without legitimacy; various forms of authoritarianism, which abuse authority; and anarchy, in which each individual is an authority to him or herself.

What is true of human community generally is true also of the church. It is not possible for the church, in its various manifestations, to exist in faithfulness to its calling without the willingness of its members to submit themselves to the authority of its deepest convictions about God, God's purposes for the world, and the church's role in those purposes. But these core beliefs and values, which bind the church together, must be articulated and interpreted in ever-changing circumstances. Conflicts must be managed. Boundaries between the church and other communities must be maintained. Directions for the church's life and work must be envisioned. All of this implies leadership, and leadership implies authority. The critical questions are not Whether authority? or Whether leaders? but What kind of authority? and What kind of leaders?

A PERSPECTIVE ON AUTHORITY

Authority is a difficult and complex concept. It is beyond my purpose to consider the various arguments about its meaning.[2] Rather, this project attempts to develop a perspective on authority as it applies to ministry, both clergy and lay. While valuable in its own right, the perspective is designed to provide a foundation for reconceiving authority in the latter chapters of this book.

Authority and power are sometimes contrasted, sometimes used interchangeably. How are they related? Power is a resource that enables individuals or groups to achieve their purposes, with or without the consent of others who are affected by its use. When a leader uses power to get her or his way without the consent of those affected, the leader is using force or coercion. In contrast, authority is legitimate power. When individuals in a group *consent* to the directives of a leader, or to the mandates of the group's constitution, or to the teachings of scripture, for example, they are acknowledging the authority—the right—of the leader, constitution, or scripture to give direction to the group's life. They submit themselves to the directives of that authoritative person or cultural object because they believe the directives to be consistent with the core values, beliefs, and purpose of the group. Individuals in the group may not always be happy with the demand for compliance, as with paying taxes or obeying a policeman's traffic directions. They may even sometimes find it necessary to comply while dissenting privately. They comply because they accept the legitimacy of the one making the demand (or because they accept the legitimacy of the demand) and believe that compliance is for the good of the whole.

Translated into terms appropriate to the church, to

have authority is to use power in ways that a congregation or other church body recognizes as legitimate, as consonant with and contributing to the basic beliefs and purposes of the church. When a pastor or lay leader exercises power legitimately—that is, acts with authority—he or she does so by directing, influencing, coordinating, or otherwise guiding the thought or behavior of others in the congregation in ways that they acknowledge as right. The congregation accepts the leader's opinions or directives as consistent with and contributing to the church's mission. The person may exercise authority in a hierarchical, top-down, authoritarian fashion that keeps the congregation dependent and submissive. Or he or she may do so in a way that acknowledges the gifts of others in the congregation and helps them to claim their own authority for ministry. In either case, so long as the group acknowledges the leader's right to exercise power, the leader is acting with authority.

The emphasis on legitimacy underscores the *relational* character of authority. Authority is not something that an individual, as an individual, possesses in the absence of a group or organization's acknowledgement that she or he has the right to exercise power. An individual may have considerable personal charisma or other important characteristics that give her or him power and the capacity to influence others. For example, the pastor may be a tall, handsome male with a deep voice and a commanding pulpit presence. While these attributes may enhance his influence and even give him power over others, they do not translate into authority unless there is some group that recognizes his exercise of power as legitimate. It can be a formal recognition, as in a written constitution, or it can be a more informal recognition, as Jesus' band of disciples demonstrated in their acceptance of his legitimacy as a leader. For clergy, ordination and a call by a congregation or assignment by a bishop are formal or institutionalized ways of conferring legitimacy.

Legitimacy as a leader also is based more informally

on a congregation or community's tacit agreement that a pastor has won the right to lead by virtue of either her or his religious authenticity or demonstrated competence or both. Authenticity and competence may have been assumed as a basis for ordination and a call, but they have to be proved in practice before a congregation or community accords the pastor full legitimacy to lead. Newly ordained clergy often experience this moment as a "second ordination," one in which the congregation accepts their legitimacy. I will return to these issues later in this chapter and the next. The point is that authority has a relational dimension. We don't possess it apart from a group or community that accords us the right to lead.

Cultural and Social Authority

Before turning to the issue of why the church grants authority, let me make one further general comment. Some discussions of authority, especially those concerned with political and legal matters, place primary emphasis on the control of behavior. While clergy and other professionals may at times try to control behavior, they are more likely to try to influence opinions and beliefs, to shape perceptions, and to affect the way that individuals define reality. In a discussion of physicians, Paul Starr (1982, 13ff.) refers to this as *cultural* authority in contrast to *social* authority.

When a pastor preaches, teaches, or counsels, she may be less interested in controlling or influencing behavior than in influencing how the others think about an issue. She is concerned to influence the person or group's way of defining reality. While this may also affect their behavior, her primary intent is shaping the others' perspective. This too is an exercise of power—legitimate power insofar as the church recognizes the right of that pastor to do so. Indeed, in a voluntary association such as the church, much of the exercise of authority by clergy and other leaders is cultural rather than social in character.

Cultural and social authority are often combined. A request for members of the congregation to give their money to support the mission of the church (an attempt to influence behavior) will likely be preceded by a sermon that interprets why they should give (the exercise of cultural authority). Members may comply with the pastor's request without the interpretation, but they are more likely to do so, and to do so more generously, if they understand its importance.

In general, most professionals' cultural authority exceeds their social authority. Neither physicians nor clergy have the coercive powers of the state to enforce compliance. The principle of voluntary association makes it highly improbable that clergy can enforce compliance with their teachings. At one time, clergy had the power of excommunication, and congregations had the power of expulsion—"shunning" the Amish call it—as means of enforcing compliance. While these means still exist in principle, they are infrequently used, and it is doubtful that they carry the same weight that they did when people accepted a more literal vision of the flames of hell—or believed in a hell at all.[3]

Clergy not only have extremely limited capacity to enforce compliance, they may actually be restricted from doing so by convention or by law. For example, Catholic bishops in the United States make clear their church's teaching opposing abortion, but they cannot enforce compliance. Indeed, in the 1988 elections, bishops came under the threat of a suit that would have removed the church's tax-exempt status if their teaching against abortion called specifically for Catholics to vote against pro-abortion parties or candidates.[4]

Finally, cultural authority can also reside in cultural objects that are the result of past intellectual activity. Thus authority resides in sacred texts such as the Bible, recognized standards of reference such as dictionaries or encyclopedias, or a foundational document such as the U. S. Constitution. These are authorities that we consult in our efforts to interpret reality or to resolve ambiguities or conflicts. This is clearly of importance for understanding clergy authority as clergy draw on the Bible as a resource in exercising leadership.

To sum up, while the clergy role includes social authority in clergy's efforts to influence behavior, much of the role involves cultural authority in efforts to give definition to reality and to discern meaning and value. In the previous chapter, I cited the judgment by Ivan Vallier that clergy are somewhat deficient in contrast to their colleagues in secular professions: "He [the clergy person] interprets while his colleagues in the secular professions prescribe; he tries to give meaning to the event, since he cannot control it." If we take seriously the difference between social and cultural authority, then interpreting rather than prescribing is not a deficiency. It is simply a different type of authority and one that may be equally as important as the authority that can prescribe action or regulate events.

BASES OF AUTHORITY

Why does a group grant authority to a leader or group of leaders? What is it that warrants their trust? Answering these questions is particularly important for understanding clergy authority.

One well-known and important answer is Max Weber's (1968, 212–271) discussion of three types of authority. Each type reflects a different basis for exercising and complying with authority. Authority may be exercised on *traditional* grounds, "resting on an established belief in the sanctity of immemorial traditions and the legitimacy of those exercising authority under them" (p. 215). Or, it may rest on *charismatic* grounds, "resting on the devotion to the exceptional sanctity, heroism or exemplary character of an individual person, and of the normative pattern or order revealed or ordained by him" (p. 215). Finally, authority may be based on *rational-legal* grounds, "resting on a belief in the legality of enacted rules and the right of those elevated to authority to issue commands" (p. 215). Weber meant these descriptions as ideal types; that is, they were an effort to describe the pure form of each. In real life, we usually find them in some combination, but with one as the dominant type. We can, nevertheless, recognize each in modern organizations, including the church.

There is authority based on time-honored traditions: "We've always done it this way and have a duty to continue to do so." Every congregation has members who have at least an informal authority as guardians of the congregation's traditions. Also, one aspect of the clergy role historically has been guardianship of the church's traditions, especially the biblical tradition.

Likewise, charisma is still a basis for granting authority, although we have trivialized its meaning by equating it with personality. Charismatic leaders usually do have strong personalities, but their charisma comes especially from a mystique based on belief in their special relationship to God or the sacred and their ability to envision a new and meaningful future. While the Hebrew prophets and Jesus are prime examples of charismatic leaders, so also was Hitler in his appeal to Germany's sacred past and his projection of a thousand-year reich.

In Weber's view, neither traditional nor charismatic authority is the dominant type in modern society. Rather, rational-legal authority, authority granted on the basis of reason or technical competence and sanctioned legally, has come to be primary. Professional authority, including that of professionally trained clergy, rests in large measure on rational-legal grounds, as we shall see.

We may recast Weber's three grounds for granting authority in a somewhat different way, which is more helpful in considering clergy authority. To begin, we must distinguish between ultimate and penultimate bases. Ultimate bases are the bedrock experiences and convictions on which authority is based. Penultimate bases are more specific ways of spelling out the qualifications for the legitimate exercise of power in a group.

The Ultimate Basis

Let me begin the consideration of the ultimate basis for granting authority by coming back to Weber. As a number of commentators (e.g., Nisbet 1966, 251ff.) have pointed out, Weber viewed charisma as more than a type of authority. It was also his way of thinking about the sacred and its relation to society, though he never spelled this out fully. For him, charisma was a manifestation of the power of that which a society or group considers sacred and thus as the ultimate source of authority.[5] Charisma, the power of the sacred, whether defined in terms of Yahweh, the Word, Allah, the Tao, the Nazis' "Blood and Soil," or the "American Way of Life," lies behind all social organization and conceptions of authority as their ultimate basis. It also lies behind conceptions of scripture or church tradition as their ultimate basis, though fundamentalists often forget this as they substitute the letter for the spirit. The sacred may be explicitly recognized and named as such—for example, God or Allah—or it may be expressed more in terms of core beliefs and values that inform the culture of a group or organization—for example, "The American Way".[6] The power that is exercised legitimately by one in authority ultimately derives from the power of the sacred or the power of the group's core convictions and beliefs. Following this line of reasoning, John Shütz, in a study of the authority exercised by the apostle Paul, defines authority as "the interpretation of power" (Shütz 1975, 14). It is not the pastor or priest's power but the power of God that he or she interprets.

This is obviously a broad, variable, and functional way of construing the sacred, but it points to the importance for social organization of some conception of the sacred, whether in terms of a transcendent God or more modestly as a set of core values and beliefs about an organization and its purpose. This is the ultimate basis of authority within a particular group. The leader is granted authority to lead because she or he is believed to protect, interpret, and represent the group's core values and beliefs and contribute to their realization. While I hold this to be true of all organizations, it is certainly true of the church and of the authority that the church grants to clergy and other leaders.

For Christians, authority (legitimate power) in the church, including clergy authority, has typically been grounded in the church's convictions about God as we know God in various historical experiences, and especially as in the history of Jesus Christ. These convictions, and the experiences on which they rest, are the ultimate source and defining character of the power that leaders exercise legitimately in the church. They are also the ultimate source of the legitimacy of other authorities such as scripture or tradition. People grant authority to scripture and the church's tradition(s)—and to those who interpret them—because they believe, in last analysis, that these authorities are grounded in God and God's purposes for the world.

This implies, of course, that there are shared convictions and experiences of the sacred as the ultimate basis of authority. For Christians this means shared convictions, not only that God is but that God's purposes can be discerned.

For some Christians this is self-evident and unequivocal, at least concerning an infallible scripture or an infallible teaching office in the church. God is. God can be known clearly in God's self-revelation in scripture and the teaching office of the church. Thus a pastor's teaching and precepts are authoritative because they can be shown to be based in God's will as clearly revealed in these infallible sources.

For many of us today, myself included, there is less certainty. Although disagreements over the character and purposes of God have marked the history of the church from its earliest days, such disagreements have become particularly acute. Recall the discussion in the last chapter of the crisis of belief brought about by our growing awareness of the historicity and relativity of all knowledge, including our knowledge of God. This awareness erodes our certainty about many of the basic convictions about God and God's purposes that many Christians through the years have held to be self-evident. We find it impossible to escape historicity by reference to an infallible scripture or an infallible church. If the Bible and the church's teachings continue to function as authorities, it is not because we believe they are infallible or have escaped the relativities of historical experience. We accept their legitimacy confessionally, not propositionally. We trust them as reliable interpreters of God's power, as reliable sources of a vision of God's purposes for the world and for human life. We believe that their teachings and precepts point beyond themselves to God and God's purposes, as difficult as these sometimes may be to discern. And this is true also for the authority we grant to clergy and other leaders of the church. We grant them authority to lead, not because they claim infallibility or cloak themselves in an infallible scripture or an infallible church, nor simply because the church has ordained some of them into the clergy office. In last analysis, we grant them authority or legitimacy because we have come to trust them as reliable representatives and interpreters of God's power and purposes.

Why do we come to trust them in these ways? How do they win legitimacy? These questions bring us to penultimate bases for exercising power in the church—that is, more specific reasons for granting authority to those who lead in the church, especially to clergy.

Penultimate Bases of Authority

A number of penultimate factors have no doubt contributed historically to the authority of religious leaders. They include such things as inheritance as a member of a priestly caste, the possession of unique physical or psychic attributes, special knowledge of a sacred tradition, charisma and exemplary sanctity, or various kinds of expertise. It is not my purpose to discuss each of the various possibilities. I have already noted some of them in the discussion of Weber's types.[7] Rather, this discussion will be restricted to two bases that are especially pertinent to the role of contemporary religious leaders: authority as representative of the sacred and the authority of expertise.[8] Having either of these bases need not exclude the other, but they have often been in serious tension, as we shall see.

Representing the Sacred

I have a sociologist friend who is a professed atheist. He is also the son of a rabbi. Although an atheist, he confessed once to what he calls an irrational, gut-level deference whenever he encounters a rabbi or priest dressed in black clerical garb. What is it about the garb that triggers his response? No doubt in large part it is a form of continued deference to his father, the rabbi. But it is also a deference, as he admits, to the power of the sacred that his father and other clergy represent—even when the son no longer believes in God. A television commercial reflects a similar deference when it depicts a father confessing to his wife and children his real reason for buying a certain car after they drive past the family's priest standing in front of the church. The priest is a symbol of the sacred, and, so implies the commercial, the sacred requires truthfulness.

While some clergy appear to invite this identification and even adopt a sepulchral voice and other gestures to symbolize their sanctity, many clergy dislike such identification and the deference it often brings. Stressing egalitarianism, some trade clerical garb for T-shirts or at least try to modernize their "clerics" by substituting bright colors for the traditional black. We want to be one of the guys or one of the girls. Try as we may, however, it is difficult for us to avoid identification as a "man or woman of God." For better or for worse, clergy are the institutionalized representatives of the sacred in society. This is a basis of the authority or legitimate power that clergy have. Let us try then to understand what it means.

As noted, authority to lead in the church is grounded ultimately in the church's convictions about God and God's purposes. A corollary, true in almost all religions, is the belief that some individuals have a special relationship to God, that they embody the power of the sacred or that they incarnate core beliefs and values. They are temporary or permanent mouthpieces through which God may speak or be present. Consequently, they are considered to be authorities—charismatic authorities, to use Weber's category. Paul's primary warrant for authority was, as we have seen, an appeal to the spiritual power that was his as a result of his calling. As Joachim Wach (1944, 34) has written, "Those enjoying religious authority are believed to live in a singularly close and intimate communion with the deity; therefore, all that pertains to this experience is primary, and all that which is related to it only indirectly is expected to take second place in the life of the *homo religiosus*."

Within the Christian tradition, there are at least two major versions of this type of religious authority: a catholic (or priestly) version and an evangelical (or pietistic) version. The two are frequently merged in practice, but there are important differences.

Giving expression to the catholic version, Urban Holmes describes the priest as a "sacramental person," a *theotokos* ("God-bearer"), a "mystagogue." "To be a mystagogue," says Holmes (1978, 67), "is to lead people into the mystery that surrounds our life . . . deepening humanity's understanding of itself by word and action, by the very nature of the priest's presence." It is not the moral character or piety of the priest, to which the evangelical version gives greater emphasis, that is important. Rather, it is the priest's status as bearer of the sacred in the midst of life. From this perspective, Holmes is sharply critical of the professional model of ministry— overly so, I believe—for neglecting the being of the minister in favor of instrumental skills. Similarly, theological education in the Catholic Church, at least since the Council of Trent in the sixteenth century, has given primary emphasis to forming the spirituality of its future priests. The Tridentine fathers established seminaries— literally, "seed plots"—where they could protect candidates from worldly influences while they nurtured them for their sacramental office. Academic concerns and pastoral skills took second place to spiritual formation into the office of priesthood. Furthermore, wearing distinctive clerical garb and maintaining celibacy have symbolized the distinctiveness of the priest as bearer of the sacred.

While evangelical Protestants (which in the nineteenth century included the majority of Protestants in the United States) would have disagreed with the sacramental theology undergirding the catholic model of ministry, they nevertheless also viewed their clergy as having a special relationship to God. It was not enough to know about God or have skills to practice ministry. At the heart of one's authority to minister was an inward call from God, a gift of the Spirit, without which one could not hope to lead others to experience God's grace. Evangelicals gave, and continue to give, much greater weight to the personal or inward call of the minister than to the clergy's sacramental or representative role.

The centrality of the inward call was at the heart of the struggle in the eighteenth century between the supporters of the Awakening, led by Gilbert Tennent, and the anti-revivalists among the Philadelphia Presbytery. Was it a sufficient guarantee of a candidate's worthiness for ministry that the candidate had received ministerial training, as the anti-revivalists generally maintained? Or should one insist on an inward call from God? Tennent's very definite answer was expressed in his classic sermon, "The Danger of an Unconverted Ministry," where, among other things, he compared an unconverted minister with "a Man who would learn others to swim before he had learn'd it himself, and so is drowned in the Act, and dies like a fool . . . ." (Smith, et al. 1960, 326).

The importance that parishioners continue to attribute to a clergyperson's closeness to God is illustrated in the following paragraph from Nancy Ammerman's study of a fundamentalist congregation (1987):

> Most members see [the pastor] only in his ritualized roles and maintain an idealized view of his character. One woman talked about how amazed she is that his sermons apply to ordinary, sinful people: "How would a man like him, who is, who is so, just so wonderful, how would he know the human traits that we people have that, that are like that? Because I'm sure he hasn't got them." Although most members know that the pastor is human and sinful, just as they are, they nevertheless see him as somewhat larger than life, a little above the messiness of the everyday world (p. 122).

Such perspectives are not confined to fundamentalists. In a liberal Protestant parish a member commented to me, "I could never go to Dr. X (the pastor) with a problem. He's so good that I'm sure he wouldn't understand." She meant that not as a criticism but as a compliment, expressing her perception of his closeness to God.

Whether authority lies in the sacramental character of the priestly office or in the personal sanctity of the evangelical preacher, both catholic and evangelical perspectives agree that the ordained person has a special relationship to God and is God's representative. There is a conviction that she or he is an instrument through which Christ is at work. This is a crucial ingredient of the respect and trust that laity accord to their leaders.

Does granting clergy authority on the basis of their special relationship to God imply something qualitatively different about clergy in contrast to laity? This issue will be addressed more fully in the next chapter. Suffice it to say here that the answer is, in principle, no; but often in practice, yes. In his study of Paul's exercise of authority, Shütz (1975) shows that the most important basis for Paul's claim to authority was his appeal to a direct relationship to the power of the crucified Christ (see 1 Corinthians 1–2; 2 Corinthians 11–13), which was present in Paul's weakness. But Paul also maintained that this power was not the special preserve of leaders such as himself. It was available to all Christians through the preaching of the gospel and through baptism into Christ.

Nonetheless, by the end of the first century the emerging, post-Pauline churches began to make distinctions between the spiritual authority of the apostles and ordinary Christians. By the fourth century, the church viewed all clergy as having a relationship to God that was unavailable to the laity. Laity became second-class spiritually, and a long history of clericalism was underway. These abuses of spiritual power notwithstanding, being a representative of the sacred in the midst of life is one important penultimate basis for a clergyperson's authority.

Expertise and Authority

The other penultimate basis of particular importance for granting clergy authority is expertise: having the knowledge and skills that the church and its members consider important resources for the ministry and mission of the church. As a penultimate basis for authority, knowledge or expertise especially reflects Weber's third type of authority, which he called rational-legal, and it is characteristic of modern professional occupations.

Expertise is nothing new as an expectation for clergy. Early in the life of the church the purity of the apostolic tradition was entrusted to presbyters (later called bishops) who were viewed as successors of the apostles. Their responsibilities also included overseeing the life of the churches in their care. In this practice, as Bernard Cooke (1975, 419) notes,

> We have the beginnings of the process by which, lacking anything like seminary formation, ministerial "know-how" was passed on by informal instruction, example, and apprenticeship. Thus, in addition to apostolic tradition in the strictest and narrowest sense, there would have been episcopal traditions of homiletics, liturgical ceremony, catechetical formation, and community organization. Proficiency in such was certainly a factor in the authority which a bishop was able to exert over his people.

While the expectation of competence was not always the case, especially for parish clergy, it received a considerable boost at the time of the Reformation. The Reformed tradition in particular, under Calvin's influence, strongly emphasized a learned ministry. The Geneva gown, a scholar's robe, became a symbol of the Reformed pastor's authority. That tradition continued among New England Puritans. Although New England laity were almost uniformly literate and most read their Bibles regularly, they nevertheless deferred to the minister's expertise in biblical interpretation. He was the one who read the Bible in Greek and Hebrew and had access to commentaries, concordances, and other books for interpretation. This particular resource was valued as an important source of his authority (Stout 1987, 32). The Puritan pastor was also expected to be an expert in pastoral discernment as he counseled with men and women who were anxious about their salvation (Holifield 1983, 81–82). Because the parishioner's eternal destiny hung in the balance, it was terribly important for the pastor to be accurate in his discernment and counsel.

While expertise had been a partial basis for granting

clergy authority from early in the church's history, it became especially so in the United States and Great Britain beginning in the early to mid-nineteenth century. During this time what many have called the modern view of professions emerged (see Bledstein 1976; Larson 1977; Russell 1980). Previously the professions—especially law, medicine, and the clergy—had been as much statuses to which one belonged by virtue of one's culture and education in a hierarchically ordered society as they were self-conscious occupational groups. As both Britain and America changed from rural and agrarian to urban and industrial societies, the older "status" professions were transformed. Along with other emerging professions, they became more specifically defined and organized occupationally to meet the specialized needs for knowledge and services in the changing society. As Bledstein (1976, x) has written, "The most emphatically middle class man was the professional, improving his worldly lot as he offered his special knowledge and services to society, expressing his expanding expectations as ascending stages of an occupation."

Also of great significance at this time was the rise of modern science and technology. It became important to the emerging professions to demonstrate that their practice was grounded in a scientifically based theory that could be translated into skills for addressing important human problems. Improving existing schools and developing new ones to educate the new professionals provided major impetus for the growth of universities and professional schools. A large number of seminaries had their start in part as a response to the new emphasis on the professionalization of ordained ministry.

Reflecting on these changes as they affected the Congregational ministry in New England, Donald Scott (1978, 145–155) calls it a move from "office to profession":

> By the 1850s, in institutional terms, the clergy had become a profession, a coherent, self-conscious oc-

cupational body, organized and defined by a set of institutions which were outside lay or public control, and which possessed the power to determine who could enter the clerical ranks. . . . Whether a pastor or not, the clergyman's essential orientation . . . was now toward the profession. It created him, sustained his sense of himself as a clergyman, defined his role and provided the most important community of which he felt himself a part and by which he distinguished himself from other groups in the society.

Of special importance to our concern with expertise as a basis for authority is Scott's observation that defining themselves as professionals enhanced the importance of their expertise and thus their authority:

Its character as a profession enhanced the clergy's collective legitimacy as the overall guardian and definer of God's word and presence in society. Under the culture of professionalism, monopoly . . . properly belonged to the collective body of certified practitioners, those who had gone through the rituals and training (which only those already through them could define and control) that made one a "professional" rather than a layman or amateur.

Under the leadership of educators such as William Rainey Harper, President of the University of Chicago, there were efforts to reform the education of ministers along more professional lines, especially by seeking a scientific basis for practice and by placing heavy emphasis on skills needed in that practice. The development of biblical criticism, efforts to develop a scientific theology, and especially the virtual explosion that occurred in the field of practical theology were among the most important late nineteenth- and early twentieth-century efforts to foster a scientific approach to ministry in theological education.

Expertise as a basis for clergy authority continues to be important. Almost all the major denominations require a seminary education or its equivalent for its ordained clergy. Those that do not face pressures, often from an increasingly educated laity, for an educated clergy.

Denominations vary in the kind of expertise that they hold to be important, depending on the denomination's dominant image or model of ordained ministry. For example, a major study of lay and clergy expectations of ordained ministers (Schuller et al. 1980) found that Presbyterians and other denominations in the Reformed tradition place great emphasis on a learned presentation of the faith; United Methodists give particularly high value to clergy's interpersonal competencies; Southern Baptists strongly emphasize skills in aggressive evangelism; and Orthodox Christians place the highest value on the priest's liturgical leadership. While these differences come as no surprise, they illustrate denominational differences in the expertise valued.

Views of needed expertise have varied historically as well. Drawing on an unpublished study by Ronald Osborn, authors Joseph Hough and John Cobb (1985) trace four models of ordained ministry that have been dominant at different times in American history. First there was the *Master* (primarily pre-nineteenth century), whose knowledge was mostly of the generalist sort expected of most cultured gentlemen. The Master was followed by the *Revivalist* or *Pulpiteer* (primarily nineteenth century), who was not only a persuasive preacher but also knew well the psychology and techniques of evangelism. Next came the *Builder*, whose expertise lay in developing and administering the large institutional churches and their diverse programs that came into being in large towns and cities in the early part of the twentieth century. Finally, there is the *Manager*, which Hough and Cobb believe is the dominant image today and which gives priority to expertise needed to run efficient organizations. They are especially critical of the latter model and the atheological stance that it often reflects. I agree with this criticism and will elaborate more fully on it in chapter 5 as I propose a model of the minister as a reflective leader. For now, note that expertise is one important basis for granting clergy authority. Whatever the particular model of ministry, having the requisite knowledge and skills to carry it out is a resource that churches value in their leaders and recognize as authoritative.

To sum up, there are at least two important penultimate bases for clergy authority: representative of the sacred (with both catholic and evangelical versions) and expertise. These two bases are distinct, but they are not mutually exclusive. While they have often been set over against each other—as in Tennent's critique of an unconverted ministry; or, similarly, in the cleavage in New England between evangelicals, gathered around Jonathan Edwards, and rationalists, gathered around Charles Chauncey; or, more recently, in the numerous criticisms of the professional model of ministry—one need not exclude the other. Indeed, one of my purposes is to show how the two together help clergy address the crisis of authority that I described in the preceding chapter. *If we have authority as clergy, it is because laity perceive us to be reliable interpreters of the power and purposes of God in the context of contemporary society. And this involves both spirituality and expertise, not one without the other.*

Personal versus Institutional Authority

There is one further distinction in this perspective on authority to which I have already alluded. It can be put in the form of a question: Does the ordained person's authority derive from the formal office of priest or pastor, which she or he enters at ordination and which also presupposes social acknowledgement? Or does the ordained person's authority derive from his or her person, that is, from some personal qualities or attributes that are socially acknowledged?

Authority of office reflects the religious group's concern to protect its sacred tradition, preserving the charisma and teachings of its founder by institutionalizing them into an office. Mircea Eliade (1959, 101) once said that "the true sin is forgetting [the myth]." Institutionalizing authority in an office that one enters at ordination is an attempt to prevent this "true sin" from occurring, as, for example, in the doctrine of apostolic succession. For Protestants belief in an infallible or even inerrant Bible is a similar attempt. Authority derives from entry into the office of priest through the laying on of the hands of those who themselves are successors to the apostles. In such a way, the church sought to preserve its Christian identity, creating a number of dilemmas in doing so.[9]

In the extreme case of authority of office, personal attributes of the clergy count for little or nothing. Authority derives solely from ordination into the clergy office. In Graham Greene's novel *The Power and the Glory* (1946), the leading character is an alcoholic priest who had lost his faith. Yet at one point, parishioners in the village where he was hiding from the police prevailed on him to celebrate Mass, since they had no other priest. Reluctantly, he agreed. Because of the authority of office into which he entered through ordination he could, as he said, "put God in their mouths" despite his own lack of a personal faith and his moral failures. This view reflects the church's decision, in the wake of the fourth-century Donatist controversy, to consider as valid the sacramental acts of an unworthy priest, whose inner motives did not affect the efficacy of the sacrament.

While the function of authority of office is to protect the sanctity of the tradition, *authority of person* guards against clergy functioning that is devoid of personal authenticity, whether of spirituality or expertise. It is based not on office but on the recognition that the clergy's personal characteristics and qualities warrant granting him or her legitimacy. Greene's whiskey priest may have been able to celebrate the Eucharist because of the priestly office in which he participated. Had he been called to serve the parish as a trustworthy interpreter of God's power and purposes, he would have had a serious problem. Or, to repeat an example I cited earlier, parishioners may grant authority to lead the congregation to a newly ordained seminary graduate (and probably to any minister who is new to the congregation) by virtue of his or her ordination. They accept the denomination's certification that he or she has the appropriate credentials. It will take time, however, for them to acknowledge his or her personal authority as a trustworthy interpreter of power based on personal characteristics and qualities—what I referred to earlier as a "second ordination." This kind of authority must be earned.

As with the distinction between sacred and expert bases of authority, authority of office and personal authority are not mutually exclusive. They are, however, often in tension, and denominations vary in the emphasis they give to one or the other.

Although not mutually exclusive, the two kinds of authority are distinct, and they often have substantively different consequences for clergy functioning. In a study of clergy involvement in social issues, Harold Quinley (1974, 276–277) found that clergy whose authority was institutionalized in an office were more likely to be involved in controversial issues than those whose authority depended more on personal attributes. The office gave them a degree of freedom that personal authority did not provide. Similarly, James Wood (1981, 75ff.) found that, when clergy had formal authority (authority of office), church members were more likely to tolerate controversial policies and practices by their denomination and clergy, even when the members personally disagreed with the policies and practices. They felt more of a moral obligation to support them than was true in denominations with congregational polities where clergy authority was based more on personal qualities and relationships than on office. Many of us who served parishes in the

South during the civil rights movement found this to be true. Those of us in denominations that emphasized authority of office generally found that we had greater institutionalized freedom to speak and act in favor of an end to segregation, even when our congregations strongly disagreed, than did our colleagues in congregationally based polities. A parishioner once commented that he disagreed strongly with me in my stand on racial justice, but he recognized my right to speak because "Nashville told me to do so"—his way of describing the Methodist Church and also, by implication, my authority of office. At the same time, many of us also found that a combination of office and personal authority made an even stronger combination. As Wood (1981, 82) notes, "Even organizations with substantial formal legitimacy need to cultivate or maintain belief in legitimacy in order to assure voluntary support." In this sense, authority of office and personal authority are mutually reinforcing.

We can combine the distinction between the two penultimate bases of authority—representing the sacred and expertise—with the distinction between authority of office and authority of person to yield four orientations of clergy authority, as in the following table:

CONCEPTIONS OF AUTHORITY

	OFFICIAL AUTHORITY	PERSONAL AUTHORITY
REPRESENTING THE SACRED	A Sacramental/ Priestly	B Personal Piety
EXPERTISE	C Certified Competence	D Demonstrated Competence

Authority as representative of the sacred can be based primarily on office, as is the case in the more sacramental or liturgical denominations (cell A). Or it can be based primarily on perceptions of the minister's personal piety, as in traditions that place most emphasis on conversion and the inward call (cell B). In their study entitled *Ministry in America,* David Schuller and his associates (1980, 45–46; 60–66) found both of these kinds of sacred authority. Members of Southern Baptist and other evangelical churches opted for a model of ministry that the authors called a "spiritual emphasis" and that included personal spirituality, ethical living, and evangelism as marks of an effective pastor. Clearly distinguishable was a second model of ministry, which the authors labeled "a sacramental-liturgical emphasis," with accent on clergy as representatives of the Holy and whose principal function is administering the sacraments. Not surprisingly, liturgical denominations—Roman Catholic, Orthodox, and Episcopal—most strongly affirm this model.[10]

We can also think of expertise in this dual fashion. One's office authority may include certification that one has requisite training, expertise in preaching, teaching, or other aspects of pastoral leadership (cell C) whether one, in fact, has the competence to do so or not. Presbyterian clergy, for example, are ordained as "teaching elders," a description of their office, whether they are effective in their teaching or not. On the other hand, one may gain personal authority by demonstrating expertise, whether it is institutionally legitimated or not (cell D). Jesus, for example, astonished the crowds by his teaching, "for he taught them as one who had authority, and not as the scribes" (Matt. 7:29). The scribes, who had office authority to teach, presumably taught by citing the tradition and other authorities, but they lacked the personal expertise and authenticity evident in Jesus' teaching. He had the capacity to make God present in the midst of human life.

A different example comes from Paul Harrison's

(1959) study of the American Baptist Convention. Baptist denominational executives had no authority of office to exercise leadership in the denominations (cell C). Nevertheless, they exercised power based on personal expertise (cell D) as they helped the autonomous Baptist churches work together to achieve common goals. Their authority was personal—Harrison called it "rational-pragmatic"—rather than official or rational-legal.

These four patterns of authority are of use primarily in sorting out differences of emphasis in various denominational traditions. Rarely are they found in the pure form. They are, however, helpful in understanding how different authority patterns contribute to some of the important tensions and conflicts that arise in the churches.

Increasingly, as noted in chapter 1, all denominations seem to be moving in the direction of congregationalism or voluntarism, even when their polities remain episcopal or presbyterian. This is true even of Catholicism. Commenting on leadership patterns in Catholic parishes, David Leege (1986, 1) summarized his findings from a major study of Catholic parishes:

> What is . . . characteristic of the modern American parish is that leadership is not simply a status but a way of doing things. Authority may reside in a position, but unless the person who occupies that position can act legitimately and effectively in the eyes of those around him, he is not viewed as a leader.

This means that personal authority has grown in importance and will continue to do so, and it makes clergy and other congregational leaders increasingly vulnerable in two ways: They may be vulnerable to the temptation to please at any price, either by "tiptoeing through tithers" or "scratching every itch" that parishioners express. They may also be vulnerable to controversy, conflict, and possible dismissal when they seek to be faithful to Christian identity as they understand it. Also, in a society such as the United States, with its sharp separation between church and state, if clergy have any legitimacy outside the church, it will be because of personal authority, not authority of office. All of this makes it imperative that we learn to lead in such a way that our personal authority is recognized and that we are trusted as reliable interpreters of God's power and purposes, even when we ask individuals to transcend their own contrary inclinations and interests. How we might do so is the subject of much of the rest of this book.

While I believe that the importance of personal authority is on the increase and it is given particular emphasis in the chapters that follow, let me simply note the danger in this trend, implied in my comment about the vulnerability of clergy. When personal authority supercedes authority of office, there is a risk of forgetting (or destroying) the myth, to recall Eliade's statement about "true sin." Both types of authority are needed, each complementing the other.

3

THE RELATIONAL DIMENSION OF AUTHORITY

"[Laity] must not . . . be flattered into an overweening estimate of their capabilities. . . . There are disputes pertaining to the nature of the will, to the relations of sin, which try the sagacity of the most sharp-sighted philosophers, and on which we should not invite the mechanic and the ploughman to pass a dogmatical decision."

—Edwards A. Park

"Every profession is a conspiracy against the laity."

—George Bernard Shaw

These statements get to the heart of the topic of this chapter: How is the authority relationship between clergy and laity structured? More specifically, how can clergy and lay leaders in the church exercise the authority that the church requires without either Park's arrogance or Shaw's cynicism? More positively, how can authority be exercised in the church so that the whole ministry of the church, ordained and lay, is empowering and empowered? These issues reflect the *relational dimension* of authority. In this chapter, I consider variations in the patterning of clergy and lay relationships over time, paying special attention to various models of ministry, including the professional model.

The Patterning of Authority Relationships

As previously stated, authority arises in social relationships. We do not have authority independent of a social group or community that authorizes or legitimates our use of power. In such groups, relationships are structured in roles that often have authority implications: parents and children, leaders and followers, professionals and clients, teachers and students, clergy and laity. The patterning of these roles—that is, the kind of relationships they involve—is what is meant by the relational dimension of authority. Such patterning can vary along a continuum. At one end there are highly *asymmetrical* authority relationships in which one of the role partners dominates the other because of unequal access to power. At the other end are highly *symmetrical* authority relationships, where there is no domination but rather an equal sharing or balance of power on the part of the role partners. The particular pattern of authority relationships at given times in the church's history reflects in large part the broader patterning of relationships in society. As theologian Avery Dulles (1978, 168) observes: "A historical study of the development of the Christian ministry would probably show that the Church in every age has adjusted its structures and offices so as to operate more effectively in the social environment in which it finds itself."

Asymmetrical Relationships

Much of the criticism of authority relationships generally and of clergy-laity relationships in particular has focused on their asymmetrical character. In various works Sigmund Freud (1961) described authority relationships as a kind of re-infantilization of the masses whereby strong political or religious authorities encouraged a return to childish dependency. While he was extremely pessimistic about the masses' ability to resist authority, Freud's goal in psychoanalysis—to oversimplify considerably—was to assist his patients to become autonomous individuals, persons who control the irrational impulses of the id by the strength of their ego. They do so by the use of reason rather than by being subject to the superego, whether in the guise of an external authority figure, conscience, or some other manifestation of authority. Various forms of humanistic psychology have tempered Freud's austere vision of the autonomous individual and in its place substituted the goal of self-realization or self-fulfillment. Philip Rieff (1966) called this "the triumph of the therapeutic," and it is very much part of the culture of "expressive individualism" or "new voluntarism" described in chapter 1. It is still also a part of the critique of asymmetrical authority relationships.

Recent criticism of asymmetry in the church has centered on the professional model of ministry. Much of this criticism is deserved. One should remember, however, that asymmetry in the patterning of clergy-laity relationships began much earlier than modern professionalism and has involved other grounds for clergy-laity differences.

The need for differentiated leadership developed rather early in the church's history, probably by the end of the first century. As the young church faced internal conflicts, as it grew in size and complexity, and as it had to come to terms with the challenge of various religious movements of the Greco-Roman environment, certain distinctive leadership functions began to emerge and become regularized.[1] While struggles over power and the authority of leaders arose early on, a major contributor to asymmetrical relationships occurred in the fourth century. The exemplary sanctity expected of clergy took on special meaning when a hierarchical understanding of ministry developed through Neoplatonic influences. Pastoral theologians began to rank people in the church according to their relative spirituality: bishops first, other clergy second, monks (laity in religious life) third, and laity—the "ordinary faithful"—last. Bernard Cooke (1975, 265f.) described these developments and comments that

> what this meant among other things is that the clergy became increasingly a separate class in Christian society; they were not "ordinary people." They were above the laity not just in the dignity of their functions within the community but in the very nature of their membership in the church. This finds its ultimate expression when the peoples begin to refer to themselves as the "head" of the church."

By the Middle Ages, the hierarchical view of ministry had come to full fruition, paralleling the hierarchy of feudal society where everything had its place in a "great chain of being." It was also ensconced within what Dulles has called the "institutional model" of the church and to a lesser extent in the "sacramental model." In the institutional model priestly authority, centered in the pope and bishops and shared by priests, is essentially authority of office and involves the right to teach, sanctify, and rule. Dulles (1978, 163) describes the asymmetry of the institutional model as follows:

> When [the priest] teaches, people are obliged to accept his doctrine not because of his knowledge or personal gifts but because of the office he holds. When he celebrates the sacraments, the priest exercises sacred powers that others do not have [e.g., "the power of the keys"]. . . . When the priest commands, he does so as one set over the faithful by

Christ, so that to resist his orders is equivalently to rebel against God himself.

The sacramental model gives less emphasis to the juridical power of the bishop or priest and more to his special sanctity as mediator between God and God's people. But it too creates asymmetry and a view in popular piety of the priest as one with supernatural powers, "as one who stays close to God so that the laity, relying on [the priest's] intercession, may be worldly,"—the reverse of what is intended, as Dulles notes (1978, 174).

The Second Vatican Council placed emphasis on the church as the people of God, which implies, as we shall see, a more symmetrical view of authority; nevertheless, the juridical and spiritual asymmetry of the institutional and sacramental models is still present in Roman Catholicism and in some high Anglican interpretations of the priesthood. It is also present in some Protestant churches where unequal power results from a view that the pastor has a special pipeline to God that gives him or her an advantage that the average layperson does not have.

Thus, exemplary sanctity as representative of the sacred has often created asymmetry in authority relationships between clergy and laity. But so also has expertise, which is the particular basis of authority for the professional model. In terms of Dulles' models of the church, expertise and the professional model of ministry have special affinity with the "herald" model, which gives interpretation and proclamation of the Word primacy over sacrament.

Shaw's comment that professions are conspiracies against the laity reminds us that professional authority has often been criticized for creating asymmetrical relationships and keeping its clients—or in the case of clergy, their congregations—in a state of dependency. Professionals' access to resources that the lay public does not have is one source of their power and a contributor to asymmetric relationships of professional dominance. The scarce resource may be expert medical knowledge that the lay public requires for its health, legal counsel that clients need to resolve disputes or obtain justice, or expertise in biblical interpretation that laity need to discern God's will. So long as laity do not or cannot have direct access to these resources, they are dependent on those who make them available, and this often increases the social distance between laity and professionals. If I am the expert in health, the law, or salvation, I not only have resources that you need but resources that you may not have, and this adds to the distance between us. Also contributing to social distance is the professional mystique that distinctive clothing or other symbols of the professional's authority contribute: the doctor's white coat and high-tech equipment, the lawyer's wig (in England) and court ceremonial, or the clergy's collar and the smells and bells of the worship experience. Likewise, professions have often fought for the right to set standards and control entry into their profession with the justification that this protects the public from charlatans. While such protection is often needed, a more cynical interpretation sees professional associations also functioning to maintain professional monopolies over the professionals' source of power. Denominational requirements for ordination have some of the same effect.

It may be that any differences in needed expertise inevitably create asymmetry regardless of the other contributing factors. This need not be negative. It simply reflects a kind of functional differentiation which gives some members of a relationship more power than others for the benefit of the whole. What critics of the professional model point to, however, are apparently deliberate attempts by professionals to cash in on these differences and thereby enhance their own status. I view such attempts under the rubric of professional*ism*: efforts to convert the professional model into an ideology to give the professional privileged status based on special expertise. Edwards Park's apparent disdain for laity in the quotation cited at the beginning of the chapter is a case in point. His comments came in mid-nineteenth century, when the so-called modern view of professions emerged. This was not, however, the first time that the ideology of professional*ism* emerged among American clergy. Let me rehearse, in an extended example, some of the immediate prehistory of modern professionalism. Not only do these events provide examples of shifting relationships between clergy and laity, but they also lend insight into issues that continue to plague us today.

An Excursus Into American Religious History

At the turn of the eighteenth century, American society was undergoing a variety of changes that were upsetting the organic relation of church and society that had been characteristic of seventeenth-century New England. In early New England, ministers were among society's elite, enjoying considerable deference and respect. As the eighteenth century progressed, not only was society becoming more worldly and fragmented as a result of the changes, but the clergy's position was also becoming less central and secure. Several social historians (see Schmotter 1973; Youngs 1976; Harlan 1980) have analyzed responses to these changes.

Some clergy sought to bolster their status by setting themselves apart from laity and conceiving of themselves as a distinct fraternity of professionals, a kind of ecclesiastical aristocracy presiding over a lay democracy.[2] Both anti-revivalist clergy in the middle colonies and their New England counterparts also gave particular emphasis to the special technical knowledge, based on long and arduous preparation, that their profession required. In Charles Chauncey's estimation, such expertise could not come simply through divine guidance. Rather, ministers had to possess "the best advantages of learning and education to accomplish them for their difficult work" (cited by Harlan 1980, 34). Also attempting to assert their authority as a distinct profession, some Massachusetts clergy sought without much success to wrest control of the selection and ordination of clergy from congregations and church councils, which included laity, and place these functions in the hands of ministerial associations.[3] When some sought to reestablish the office of ruling elder (lay officials who stood between the congregation and the clergy and assisted the clergy in governance) many clergy resisted these efforts as an infringement on their authority. David Harlan (1980, 45) cites the particularly interesting response of John Hancock, pastor of First Church in Lexington, Massachusetts, from 1698 to 1752. When his parishioners asked him to install two ruling elders, he agreed to do so and told the congregation that he knew exactly what the new officers should do:

> I should like to have one of them come up to my house before meeting on Sunday and get my horse out of the barn, and then saddle him and bring him up to the door, and hold the stirrup while I get on. The other may wait at the church door and hold him while I get off; then, after meeting, he may bring him up to the steps. This is all of my work I can ever consent to let the ruling elders do for me.

Harlan comments that at that point the matter was dropped and no ruling elders were appointed!

These examples point to the efforts of some New England clergy to close ranks against laity. Indeed, as Youngs (1976, 91) notes, among some there was a not-so-subtle identification of the church with the ordained ministry. Using the phrase a "City set upon a Hill," which John Winthrop had meant as a description of all New England, Thomas Foxcroft declared in a 1726 ordination sermon: "Ministers are (as Parents in the Family) in a somewhat elevated and conspicuous Station; they are as a City set on a Hill, which can't be hid."

Efforts like these, designed to heighten clergy status in the face of changes, were not successful. They were opposed by many clergy themselves who argued for mutuality, as Benjamin Colman of Boston did: "[Ministers] are given *for the people* and *to* the people; not *they* formed into congregations and churches for the sake of ministers" (Harlan 1980, 41). Furthermore, laity were not powerless in the face of clergy status aspirations. Many soundly criticized pretentious clergy and opposed their efforts to concentrate power in their own hands. Youngs (1976, 102) quotes a strong criticism in the *New England Courant* of the clergy's involvement in a smallpox epidemic in Boston. The editor, James Franklin, accused clergy of basing their actions and statements on an infallible ministerial character: "Religion derives its authority from GOD alone, and will not be kept in the consciences of Men by any Humane Power." Laity also exercised their power by controlling the process of calling a pastor to a local congregation and by setting clergy salaries. And, when all else failed, they had the power of dismissal, a serious blow to a pastor's career in a time when most clergy settled as pastors of a single congregation for their entire ministry.

The influence of laity increased significantly as a result of the Great Awakening, which enfranchised laity with a new sense of their own spiritual power. At the same time, clergy also experienced a renewed sense of legitimacy. It came not from a recovery of the status of an elite office but from a new emphasis on pastoral care and leadership, which the Awakening made necessary. The Awakening, as Youngs (1976, 136) comments,

> forced the Congregational clergymen to place a new emphasis upon the more mundane, but more stable, source of their power, their ability to work with laymen. Although the activities of religious enthusiasts [often traveling evangelists such as George Whitefield] constitute the most dramatic events of the revival period, it was usually the settled pastors who guided the revival in their parishes and counseled

the people who had experienced religious awakenings. When the violent passions of the Awakening subsided, the pastor remained with his people and continued the work of nourishing religious awareness in the midst of a secular world.

In the categories of the preceding chapter, the clergy found that personal authority, based on effective pastoral care, became more important for their legitimacy than authority of office.

Harlan makes a similar point about clergy associations. Many clergy had hoped in vain that such associations, which excluded laity, would give clergy power in various ecclesiastical matters. Their real impact, however, was as what we today would call "support groups," which overcame clergy isolation, and as settings for hammering out consensus on theological issues and developing strategies for dealing with serious matters of pastoral care and discipline. Such benefits did not enhance the clergy's authority of office, but they strengthened the clergy's pastoral effectiveness and therefore their personal authority.

Regrettably, these moves to more symmetrical relationships that the Awakening fostered were short-lived. Donald Scott (1978) has analyzed the period from about 1750 to 1850, which followed the First Awakening and incorporated both the birth of the new nation and the Second Awakening.[4] I will not summarize his argument here except to note that the changes that had begun to undermine the traditional place of the New England clergy in the early eighteenth century accelerated. Tensions erupted over the role of the church—and especially the pastor—in public life. Evangelical piety, sparked by the First Awakening and rekindled in the Second, led to what some have called the "Great Reversal" and the split between "public" and "private" Protestantism (see Marty 1970; Moberg 1972). Lay expectations for the clergy role were increasingly focused on the conversion of individuals and personal attention to lay needs through pastoral visitation and various church programs. Involvement by the churches or clergy in public issues, especially abolition, was strongly discouraged and became a fertile source of conflict. Furthermore, to meet the needs of the rapid growth of churches, new recruits to the ministry often came not from traditional high status families, including clergy families, but from the lower classes and from rural areas. They lacked the status that earlier clergy had by birth.

The upshot of these and other changes was to make clergy authority much more that of person than of office; and because personal authority must always be earned, it became all the more fragile and precarious. Clergy had regularly to prove themselves to maintain their positions. Their relationship with laity became asymmetrical in the opposite direction, with laity holding the balance of power. Laity were now the clergy's clients, and clergy often complained that they were reduced to the status of mere hirelings, which in fact was the view of some laity. Recall the farmer's comment to French philosophe Crèvecoeur, cited in chapter 1, that clergy are hired hands.

It was in this ethos that the modern notion of clergy as a profession developed. In a new and self-conscious way, and as an effort to reestablish their authority, evangelical clergy began to refer to themselves as professionals (along with doctors and lawyers) implying, as Scott (1978, 128) notes, "a special area of circumscribed competence which required specific and rigorous formal training," typically in the new seminaries that were founded during the period. Scott says that what this really meant was the acceptance by clergy and laity of the idea that " 'edification' was the essential job of the minister and of a client-oriented notion of the ties between the pastor and his people" (p. 128). Social activism, uninspiring theological disquisitions, and partisanship in the Old School–New School doctrinal controversies were no longer construed as being within the bounds of pastoral responsibility. If the pastor engaged in social issues, it was as a private citizen, not by reason of the authority of the pastoral office. When he preached, he preached to aid laity in the practical conduct of life. He "preached religion rather than about it" (Scott, 129). And he left doctrinal controversies to the faculty members of newly established seminaries.

While these changes left the pastor at a considerable distance from his predecessors, the new conception of the pastoral role restored a measure of pastoral authority. It had two dimensions: expertise in a circumscribed sphere of life and a manifest Christian piety and decorum. Let me again quote Scott (p. 131): "As someone formally educated in the various theological and biblical 'sciences' in ways that no layman (no matter how learned) could be, the minister possessed knowledge that distinguished him from the laity in the same way that possession of the requisite 'science' distinguished the lawyer and doctor from the nonpractitioner." The claim to such expertise over against the laity is clear in the quotation from Edwards Park that opened this chapter. Additionally, the new clergy professional conducted his life with a bearing that would stamp him as a true minister. This included "both the morality expected of a clergyman and also the tranquility that a life in Christ's bosom brought to one" (p. 131). Scott concludes:

> The new conception of the pastor . . . surrounded the minister with an aura of professional expertise and Christian character that enforced deference to him in matters touching upon his carefully circumscribed sphere. It served to preserve him from any implication in the ordinary life of his community that might jeopardize his position, and it restored a form of authority that simple occupancy of the office had once provided (1978, 132).

This somewhat extended example of changing relationships between clergy and laity has been given, primarily, to illustrate how the balance of power has shifted back and forth, creating asymmetry in both directions. Such shifts have continued to occur, although those shifts will not be treated here. Suffice it to say that many of the current tensions over clergy authority described in chapter 1 are present in the examples cited. Moreover, many of the seeds of present-day tensions were sowed in the changes that occurred in the mid-nineteenth century.[5]

I also hope that I have made clear how professionalism, whether of the earlier or more recent version, has been an important strategy by which clergy have attempted to respond to changes and enhance their status. Readers will have surely recognized that the two strategies that nineteenth-century clergy took as the bases of their authority, expertise and piety, are a way of defining the two penultimate bases of authority discussed in the preceding chapter. Given the rather negative view of the professional model that some of these illustrations involve, does this imply a general negation of the professional model? The professional model has much to commend it, including appropriate redefinitions of the two bases of authority that nineteenth-century clergy emphasized. One does not have to agree to the nineteenth-century interpretations of expertise and exemplary piety to recognize these as important bases of authority. What are negative are attempts to use either or both of these bases as weapons to enhance clergy status at the expense of laity. But this is to get ahead of the story. Let us consider first symmetrical authority relationships.

SYMMETRICAL RELATIONSHIPS

In *symmetrical* authority relationships, power within an organization such as the church is, in principle, available to all members. In the extreme case, no one member has authority over others. All share equally in power and have the right to exercise it. There are no leader-follower or clergy-laity distinctions. Such totally symmetric relationships are much more rare organizationally than asymmetrical relationships, and the church is no exception. The development of formal leadership roles quite frequently moves them away from the symmetrical pole of the continuum by necessity. There are, however, organizations and expressions of the church with *relatively* symmetrical relationships. Sometimes this simply represents a balance of power which leads to a kind of stand-off between leaders and followers or clergy and laity. More positively, however, there are church organizations where clergy and lay distinctions are functional rather than substantive. Each has authority within the organization that supplements and complements the other's, and both exercise authority for the good of the whole. Neither's authority depends on keeping the other dependent in the way that Freud, for example, feared.

Symmetrical relationships, which also include those *relatively* symmetrical, are particularly likely to occur in churches that express what Dulles (1978) called the communal model of the church—the church as "mystical communion." The church is not an institution but rather a communion of women and men formed by the Holy Spirit that expresses itself in mutually interdependent relationships of concern and assistance. Images of the church as the body of Christ and the people of God have captured the relative symmetry of the communal model. The image of the church as household, which Letty Russell has developed in her book *Household of Freedom* (1987), is another way of expressing both the communal model of the church and the partnership and mutual interdependence characteristic of symmetrical relationships.[6] Feminist interpretations, such as Russell's, are similarly linked to Dulles' fifth model, the servant model, which also emphasizes symmetrical relationships and mutuality both within the church and outside, especially in the church's identification with the poor and oppressed in their struggle for liberation.

In many respects Paul's vision of the church, which he tried to maintain in the communities that he founded, reflects a symmetrical emphasis as far as leadership is concerned. Despite evidence of Paul's captivity to the patriarchical culture of his time, with its hierarchical views of male-female and master-slave relationships, he also leans strongly towards symmetrical relationships in his understanding of the church and its leadership, as in Galatians 3:27–28. There Paul asserts that, for those baptized into Christ, "There is neither slave nor free, there is neither male nor female; for you are all one in Christ Jesus." Within the Pauline congregations there appear to have been differentiated roles based on spiritual gifts or charisms. These, however, were not formal offices. Rather, Paul believed that all Christians, including those with particular leadership roles, share equally in charisma, the power of the gospel that God gives through the Holy Spirit. His well-known description of the church as the body of Christ in 1 Corinthians 12, in which the different parts contribute to the good of the whole, makes this clear. All leadership roles are charisms given for the building up of the body in love, as the author of Ephesians (see 4:1–16), expressing a Pauline point of view, put it.

Even more radically symmetrical were relationships in the early Christian churches associated with the Gospel of John and the Johannine epistles. As Eduard Schweizer (1961) has shown, John's is a radically charismatic view of the church. Each Christian is "born of the Spirit" and in direct and complete union with Jesus Christ, whose love is a continuing gift that guides the church's inner and outer life. There is no need for any kind of special ministry, and there are no differences in the gifts of the spirit to individual believers. The only examples of "offices" in John's Gospel or in the Johannine epistles are described as expressions of the Antichrist or enemies of God.

When the early churches established formal leadership roles in the face of growing complexity and the threat of heretical movements, these were primarily functional in character and thus relatively symmetrical. As Edward Schillebeeckx (1981, 46) has written of the first three centuries of church life: "For all its pluriformity the ministry in the church is essentially collegiality, i.e. solidarity of Christians equipped with different charismata of ministry." Only later, perhaps as late as the fourth century, did status differences between clergy and laity assume an ontological or substantive character. I do not mean to suggest that there were not strong leaders earlier whose authority was greater than that of others, which was therefore asymmetrical. Indeed Peter, Paul, and James, for example, played major leadership roles, as is clear from New Testament documents. Post-apostolic leaders did so as well. The pastoral epistles, 1 and 2 Timothy and Titus, reflect a much more hierarchical ministry structure. Nevertheless, the churches continued to view ministry as the calling of all Christians. The authority differences that existed, however asymmetrical they sometimes were, were primarily functional in character.

The early church pattern influenced Protestant reformers' teachings about the priesthood of all believers. While most retained functional distinctions between clergy and laity, the reformers taught that all Christians were called to the church's ministry of service in the world. The left wing of the Reformation, notably the Quakers and Anabaptists, carried symmetrical relationships to their extreme expression. Quakers abolished the office of clergy altogether and viewed all Christians as having equal access to the power and leading of the Spirit, much as in the Johannine books of the New Testament. The Anabaptists viewed authority as belonging to the entire community. While there were prophets and other leaders, their legitimacy rested on the acknowledgment of the community in which final authority rested.

A somewhat analogous situation is described in a study of present-day Pentecostal sects in Chile (Willems

1967). Some sects provide a striking example of symmetry where spiritual power belongs to the community. Leaders are those whom the community recognizes as having a special inspiration from the Spirit. At any time, however, a congregational member may challenge the leader, claiming a new inspiration. If the member's challenge is sustained, then she or he takes the leader's role, or a schism occurs. Much as was the case for Anabaptists, the Latin American sects represent an egalitarian reaction against the hierarchical ordering of the dominant society and against the traditional institutional model of Roman Catholicism.

AUTHORITY RELATIONSHIPS IN TODAY'S CHURCH

Where are we today in the patterning of authority relationships? As I have suggested, for both Protestants and Catholics the emphasis, often belied in actual practice, is on symmetry in clergy-laity authority relationships. This seems true whether we consider the "People of God" emphasis of the Second Vatican Council, the various forms of liberation theology that are strongly egalitarian in emphasis, or the more general emphasis on mutual or shared ministry across many denominations. In reflecting on his study of Catholic parishes, Leege (1986, 1) concluded that " 'leadership' is a plural noun. While the pastor is still central to the understanding of leadership, there are many other influential and effective people who share responsibility for the direction of the parish." African-American churches exhibit similar movement. As noted earlier, authority relationships in the African-American churches have traditionally been asymmetrical, with the pastor exercising considerable power. This too is changing in the direction of symmetry as rising levels of education and the growth of a stable African-American middle class create greater pressures from laity for a share in decision making.

It is not surprising that these changes are occurring.

Quite apart from any theological reasons, they reflect the widespread emphasis on egalitarian values in the broader culture in which the church exists. It is within an ethos whose watchword is "question authority" that we—clergy and laity alike—must learn to exercise authority in the church.

Yet, quite apart from cultural demands, the core teachings of our faith point us in the direction of symmetry. As I will argue in the following chapter, the church needs differentiated leadership, and this often leaves some "more equal" than others. Yet Jesus' example of servant leadership (see John 13:1–16) and, in the spirit of Jesus' example, Paul's organic image of the church as the body of Christ (1 Corinthians 12), both reflect a nonhierarchical, symmetrical perspective. This perspective seems to be at the heart of the gospel teaching about leadership. Thus the gospel, and not just the cultural context, moves us in the direction of symmetry and a complementarity of gifts within the ministry of the whole people of God. Achieving this is no mean task! In the chapters that follow, I try to point to some ways that it might be accomplished.

4

AUTHORITY
AND ECCLESIOLOGY

"Now you are the body of Christ and individually members of it."

—1 Corinthians 12:27

"War is too important to be left to the generals."

—Georges Clemenceau

In the preceding chapters, I have tried to develop a perspective on authority for ministry, especially that of ordained ministers. In doing so, I took note of a number of challenges that make all authority problematic, especially clergy authority. I then attempted to develop an understanding of authority from the perspective of sociology, and I used a variety of examples to show both how authority has been differently interpreted and exercised in the history of the church. From this base I propose, in the remaining chapters, to reinterpret the meaning of authority and leadership in the church in such a way that addresses the challenges to authority that we face today. The issue for the church, as I indicated in chapter 2, is not Whether authority? or Whether leaders? but What kind of authority? and What kind of leaders? What I shall describe as "reflective leadership" is my answer to these questions.

In this chapter and the next, I want to lay a basis for my reinterpretation, first by indicating in broad strokes some normative assumptions that I make about the church and its ministry, and second, in the following chapter, by describing the core leadership tasks that the church requires.

The Church's Story and the Christian Story

When Paul used the metaphor "the body of Christ" to describe the church, he was primarily concerned with organic relationships among the different "members" of the one body. But the metaphor also describes the character and calling of the church: It is the body of *Christ*. Its character and calling—and thus also the character and calling of its leaders—are defined by the story of Jesus Christ, by his life, ministry, death, and resurrection. This is my first and basic assumption about the church.

What, more precisely, does this mean? As I have expressed it elsewhere (Carroll 1988, 59), what is involved is a form of continuing incarnation of the Word. In *the* incarnation, the Word became enfleshed in a distinctive person, Jesus, the son of Mary and Joseph; in a particular place, Nazareth in first-century Palestine; and in the distinctive culture of that time and place, with its particularities of culture in first-century Middle Eastern culture and society, with its language and patterns of thought. This is the decisive incarnation of the Word and the norm that continues to inform future embodiments. However, such embodiment, indeed enculturation, meant that Jesus, the Word, accepted the opportunities and limitations that those particularities of place, culture, and society imposed. While in one sense this set limits on the Word, it also particularized it in such a way that it could be heard, understood, and responded to by real flesh-and-blood men and women who lived under the constraints of their own historicity. Rather than freeing the Word from these particular constraints so that it could become universal, the resurrection actually freed it to become particular again and again as the body of Christ in different times and places and under different historical circumstances. So Christ is incarnate in communities of Christians in first-century Ephesus, Corinth, or Rome as well as in late twentieth-century Lagos, Boston, Bloomfield, or Essex Junction. The history of the church, beginning with the New Testament congregations, is the struggle—successes and failures—of concrete communities of Christians who have tried to embody the Word with integrity in their corporate and individual lives in ways appropriate to the myriad societies and cultures in which they have lived.

The challenge to the church and its leaders in every generation is to discover in the shape of that primary embodiment—Jesus' ministry, death, and resurrection— a *praxis* that is faithful to Jesus' identity in ever-changing circumstances. I do not mean by this that we follow Jesus in a literal, step-by-step way. Rather, it is the *shape* of Jesus' story, not its precise content, that continues to shape the practice of the church. It gives us some criteria by which we can assess whether our own churchly forms and responses are Christianly apt, to use David Kelsey's phrase (1975, 192f.).[1] With reference to individual behavior, Alasdair MacIntyre (1981, 201) has said, "I can only answer the question, 'What am I to do?' if I can answer the prior question, 'Of what story or stories do I find myself a part?' " The same is true for the church. Jesus' story illumines and judges the story of God's people who came before and after that pivotal event, and it illumines and judges our own ongoing struggle to live faithfully within that narrative in the ever-changing and complex circumstances in which we find ourselves.

I risk considerable oversimplification by doing so, but let me indicate briefly some of the characteristics of

Jesus' story that I find helpful as criteria for assessing the faithfulness of the church's practice. I do so with the caution that they are not a list of principles that reduce one's need to "test the spirits" in ever-changing circumstances. I also recognize that others will nuance them differently, based on their reading of Jesus' story. Each of us must develop our own understanding of them as part of our vision of ministry, as I will discuss in chapter 7. Nonetheless, these provide one way of stating the central tendencies of Jesus' story that have implications for the tasks of the church and its leaders.

First, Jesus' ministry called all people into a new and liberating relationship with God. Jesus' identification with the poor and oppressed, clear from the start of his ministry; his love expressed in acts of healing and service; his opposition to oppressive structures; his teaching about God's character—these were all aimed at freeing men and women to participate in a new relationship with God that gave their lives meaning and restored their self-worth.

Second, Jesus taught by word and act that the new relationship with God calls men and women into a new community with one another as God's people, as brothers and sisters in the kingdom or commonwealth that God is bringing into being. These new relationships, defined by love (forgiveness, mutuality, and active concern for the neighbor), challenge and relativize traditional structures and patterns of relationships that perpetuate inequality and oppression.

Third, Jesus called and empowered his followers to share in his ministry, to be witnesses to these new relationships with God and with each other, and to call others to join them in God's commonwealth. His community of followers was given the gift and resources to continue his ministry "to the ends of the earth."

These three central tendencies are a way of summing up, as Paul did, the primary thrust of Jesus' life and ministry: "In Christ God was reconciling the world to himself, not counting their trespasses against them, and entrusting to us the message of reconciliation" (2 Cor. 5:19b). The three do not prescribe concrete behavior; rather, they describe the shape of Jesus' story, indicating different aspects of God's reconciling activity in Christ by which we may test our practice in different times and places and under changing circumstances: Does it enable men and women to enter a new relationship with God that gives their lives meaning and purpose? Does it call them to a new sense of belonging in a community based on forgiveness, mutuality, and concern for the neighbor? Does it empower members of the community to live as the people of God in the world?

MEANING, BELONGING, AND EMPOWERMENT

Although we must discover for ourselves, in concrete situations of practice, what it means to participate in Jesus' continuing story, I make a second assumption that the church functions as a community of meaning, belonging, and empowerment. These functional categories provide reminders of different but related dimensions of the church's task. To be sure, other communities also provide meaning, belonging, and empowerment to their members—for example, one's family, or one of the many "twelve steps" groups that have adopted the techniques of Alcoholics Anonymous. Yet these three functional categories take on a particular shape in the life of the church insofar as the church participates in Jesus' story. That is, his story defines the meaning that the church provides. It gives shape to a church's structures of belonging in which members participate. And it is his spirit that empowers and directs the church's members in their ministries. Since these are not typical ways of describing the tasks of the church, let me expand on them.

As a *community of meaning*, the church provides a context in which we can understand our lives and experiences in light of God's self-revelation in history, preeminently in Jesus' story. Our individual lives and our common life as members of a global village are filled with difficult, confusing, and contradictory experiences that regularly challenge us to the very roots of our being: crises occasioned by life cycle transitions; experiences of illness, suffering, and death; difficult value choices; marriage and family tensions; issues of work and vocation; issues of injustice and oppression; international tensions and conflicts; and environmental crises. Unless we hide our heads ostrich-like in the sand, we cannot avoid the individual and corporate challenges that such experiences bring. One core task of the church, therefore, is to enable us to face and respond to these crises and challenges, which threaten the fabric of our existence. The church as a community of meaning provides a context in which we are helped to interpret our stories and experiences in light of a common *memory* (the stories of Israel, of Jesus, of God's people down through the years) and a common *hope* (God's reign of justice and peace). Interpreting our experiences in light of this memory and vision helps us to make sense of our life in a transcendent context and discern, however dimly, opportunities for ministry in both the routine and extraordinary occasions of our lives. This is why vital, prophetic preaching, teaching, and pastoral guidance are so central to the church's gathered life.

The church is also a *community to which we belong*, providing relationships and structure through which we can experience acceptance, care, and support as we deal with issues of meaning and discover what it means to live as God's people. This is implied in the root meaning of religion, taken from *religo*, "to bind together."

The "binding" task of the church runs counter to the individualism and isolation of contemporary life by incorporating individuals into the commonwealth of God (for example, in baptism); by breaking down the dividing walls which separate us and calling us to new depths of relationships with each other as brothers and sisters in Christ (for example, in the Eucharist); and by nurturing us in the virtues of Christian life, the fruits of the Spirit of which Paul writes in Galatians. Let me use a personal analogy. When I went off to college, rather than giving me a list of do's and don'ts, my mother gave me only one bit of advice: "Remember who your father is." In this, she reminded me of the character of the family to which I belonged, symbolized in my father's character, and asked me to be faithful to it. Visits home for weekends were not simply pleasant reunions with family and friends. They were also occasions for experiencing acceptance, care, and support and for recalling once again who my family was and what we stood for. Belonging to the church has a similar function: incorporating us into the family of God, binding us together, and renewing our identity as God's people. It also strengthens the plausibility of the meaning of the faith, as I will emphasize in the following chapter. This core task highlights the significance of various aspects of community building—the sacraments, pastoral care, fellowship opportunities, leadership and administration, conflict management.

The first two tasks that characterize the gathered life of the church are not ends in themselves. Rather, they are means that contribute to a third core task of the church, a *community of empowerment*. Emile Durkheim, the French sociologist who interpreted religion in terms of its functions, gave particular emphasis to the belonging function of religion in contrast to beliefs or meaning. In doing so, he concluded that

> Believers . . . who lead the religious life and have a direct sensation of what it really is, . . . feel that the real function of religion is not to make us think, to enrich our knowledge . . . but rather, it is to make us act, to aid us to live. The believer who has communicated with his god is not merely a man who sees new truths of which the unbeliever is ignorant;

he is a man who is *stronger*. He feels within him more force, either to endure the trials of existence, or to conquer them (1915, 463–464).

Let me put Durkheim's functional perspective in Christian categories. As we are helped to give meaning to our experiences in terms of the Christian story and vision, as we are supported and nurtured in the common life of the church, we are also empowered, corporately and individually, to participate in the continuing ministry of Jesus in the daily rounds of our lives—work, play, family life, community, nation, globe. These, and not the gathered congregation, are the primary settings in which God calls us to ministry. The church is not only a community where one experiences meaning and belonging, it is also a community where participants are empowered to engage in ministry.[2]

There is a striking passage in Ezekiel 47, where God shows the prophet a vision of the temple in Jerusalem. Streaming out of the temple is a river that flows through the land down to the sea. Wherever it flows, it brings life. It refreshes the land, allowing animals to live and trees bearing fruit to grow. It makes the stagnant water fresh again and full of fish. The vision makes clear that the life and activities of the temple are not ends in themselves. Rather, the temple is where renewal and empowerment begin, but its gathered life leads back to the world outside the temple as those who have been renewed and empowered become agents of renewal and empowerment in their scattered lives in the world. Gathering and scattering describe, therefore, the necessary rhythm of the Christian's life.

This way of construing the church's mission also provides a way of thinking about the specific roles of ordained ministry: as interpreters of meaning, as community builders, and as supporters of public ministry. I will return to these images of the ordained role in the next chapter.

MINISTRY, THE SERVICE OF
THE WHOLE PEOPLE OF GOD

A third assumption about the church, noted earlier, is that ministry is the service to which God calls all Christians, laity and clergy. Every Christian is called, by virtue of a common baptism, to use his or her distinctive gifts for the service of God in the world. This is the church's way of expressing the truth of Clemenceau's aphorism, "War is too important to be left to the generals."

If there is one area in which almost all Christian communions, Protestant and Catholic, have reached consensus in recent years, it has been in this inclusive conception of ministry. To be sure, serious differences in the understanding of ordained leadership remain, but there is broad agreement that ministry belongs to the whole people of God. Not only is this the focus of Catholic teaching in Vatican II, but also the World Council of Churches' document, *Baptism, Eucharist and Ministry* (1982, 21) sounds a similar note: "The word ministry in its broadest sense denotes the service to which the whole people of God is called, whether as individuals, as a local community, or the universal Church." Similarly, to cite but one other example, a recent Lutheran statement on ministry (Lutheran Church in America 1984, 15) says simply that "ministry is God acting through the people of God for the life of the world."

The Lutheran statement is particularly significant in its emphasis on the life of the world as the setting for ministry. When ministry gets identified only with the gathered community where clergy have a primary leadership role, laity tend to identify ministry with what clergy do. As we have seen, clergy often have aided and abetted laity in making this identification. As one Episcopal rector expressed it, "We clergy are so addicted to being clergy—running the church and holding the power of the sacraments—that we are often unable to take the ministry of the laity seriously." As a consequence laity become, at best, a supporting cast and, at worst, the audience that is entertained and edified by the star—the "real" minister. And, of course, if they do not like the performance, they can always hire a new lead actor. If, however, we take seriously the claim that *real ministry* is "God acting through the people of God for the life of the world," a very different drama (to keep the theatrical imagery) is enacted. The lead actors are the laity whose stage for ministry is not primarily in the gathered community but in the world—in the family, the community, on the job, in politics, in all those places where lay ministers find themselves in their daily round of existence.

Earlier Ezekiel's temple image was used as a way of thinking about the rhythm of the church's life. Actually, the New Testament interpretation of the temple is even more radical. In a provocative biblical study of the laity in New Testament perspective, Thomas Gillespie (1978, 13–33) shows how the New Testament writers transformed the temple imagery of Judaism. Rather than a building or sacred place, the temple becomes a sacred people, "a royal priesthood, a holy nation, God's own people, that you may declare the wonderful deeds of him who called you out of darkness into his marvelous light" (1 Peter 2:9). The priests of this new temple are not the clergy alone but the whole people of God. Gillespie sums up his analysis as follows:

> God's "dwelling" upon earth is a people rather than a building, a holy people "set apart" for God rather than from the world, a people mandated to mission rather than coddled in seclusion, a people called by God to the living of salvation in the matrix of everyday life rather than delivered from life's cares and responsibilities, a people who live "before God" at all times and in all places rather than lead double lives in segregated sacred and secular compartments.

In a discussion of lay ministry, a layperson spoke of his ministry in just such a way: "If our desk can be our altar", he said, "our office a sanctuary, and our fellow workers our co-celebrants, then the work place can be a God place."[3]

Gillespie concludes that the vision of shared ministry "will be realized only if the 'nonclergy' are willing to move up, if the 'clergy' are willing to move over, and if all God's people are willing to move out" (p. 32). This suggests how difficult this vision is to realize. I remind the reader of the conclusion, cited earlier, from the large survey of laity by David Schuller and his associates (1975, 73): "In spite of accent within recent years on the work of 'the whole people of God,' many in the congregation still view themselves primarily as spectators rather than ones mutually called to share a ministry with others." Or, as one layperson expressed it pungently: "My task in the church is to show up, sit up, pay up, and shut up." (The Catholic version of the lay role is "to pray, pay, and obey.") These attitudes remind us that a major challenge still exists to help laity acknowledge their calling and authority for ministry and find the guidance and support to exercise their calling as God's priests in their daily lives. An equal challenge exists for clergy to learn how to exercise their distinctive roles as guides and supporters of lay ministry, seeing this to be at the heart of their particular vocation rather than as a threat to their authority.

ONE MINISTRY, DIFFERENT GIFTS

A fourth assumption about the church is: Sharing the ministry does not imply a sameness of functions. The apostle's metaphor of the body of Christ in 1 Corinthians 12 does not refer specifically to clergy-laity relationships in the modern sense—there were no clergy at the time. At the same time, it clearly recognizes the need for a differentiation of functions within the body for its own health. As Paul makes clear, one function is not more important than the other. In the organic wisdom of the body, each member is mutually supportive of the other and contributes to the fulfillment of the body's purpose: building up the community in Christ for participation in Christ's ongoing ministry of liberation and reconciliation.

How do the ministries of clergy and laity differ? I have already suggested that the primary locus of lay ministry is not the gathered community. As Celia Hahn (1985, 50) puts it graphically: "When the salt of the earth is stuck to the saltcellar, we're all in trouble!" To be sure, laity have gifts of ministry that are critical for the life of the gathered church and without which it could not survive. These, nevertheless, are secondary to laity's primary roles in the scattered life of the church. Conversely, I believe that the primary locus where clergy exercise their ministry is in the gathered community. By no means is it limited there. I am not proposing that we "baptize" the nineteenth-century curtailment of the clergy's public role by making clergy chaplains to the private sphere, but I do believe that clergy have primary responsibility for leadership within the gathered community. The key to working out these different callings is mutuality and interdependence, where each respects and supports the other's calling and authority for ministry. It is a joint enterprise, a covenantal relationship, to which clergy and laity are called.

Since this book is primarily for and about clergy, much of the rest of it will focus on the clergy role and how we might understand clergy authority and responsibilities in a new and meaningful way. However there is more to say about the lay role. Just as clergy have authority for ministry, so also do laity. Though the roles and responsibilities for which they are authorized differ, the bases of their authority are at least formally similar. That is, they are similar in form if not in specific content, which varies with the distinctive roles and the settings in which they are exercised, whether in the gathered church or outside. Recall the discussion in chapter 2 of bases of authority, which focused especially on clergy authority. How does it apply to authority for lay ministry?

As emphasized in the earlier discussion, the ultimate ground for authority in the church, whether of ordained or lay ministry, is participation in the power of God as we know God in Jesus Christ. All Christians share in this power as the ultimate basis of their charisms and the defining characteristic of their exercise of ministry as they use their gifts. This means that the power of God that energizes the ministries of clergy and laity is a gift to the whole community, not just to the ordained leader. Thus, there is no difference in the ultimate ground of authority for laity or clergy.

The two penultimate bases of authority, expertise and relationship to the sacred, also have applicability to authority for lay ministry. As clergy authority is based in part on competence for their special roles, there is no less need for laity to be competent in their particular ministries. By competence, I mean knowledge of their faith *and* the capacity to discern its relationship to their particular spheres of ministry. It is why we must understand the church as a community of meaning. In an essay entitled *The Authority of the Laity*, Verna Dozier (1982, 9f.) put the need as follows:

> Lay people need to be experts both in their own vocational area and in theology. Laity really need to know what God has done in Christ, as profoundly as any ordained minister; and they need to know their own discipline. Clergy need to know that there *are* other areas of expertise. But clergy do not need to be experts in those areas. . . . It is the task of the clergy to be sure that the people with whom they work *do* know what their faith is all about. Clergy are called to be rabbis. Rabbis do not profess to have any more spiritual genius than the congregation; they merely profess to have the learning. The learn-

ing that lay people themselves need is really not
academic learning. No lay person has to know
Greek or the history of the Church or all the arguments that the church fathers put forward. They do
need to know the gospel story. The training of the
clergy should give them a set of tools for helping lay
people know that story, the story of the people
of God.

Clergy also need the capacity to help laity discern the
relation of the Christian story to their particular voca-
tional spheres.

Lay authority also is grounded in the second penultimate basis, relationship to the sacred. In chapter 2 it
was noted that, in practice, we have often contrasted the
spirituality of clergy and lay spirituality. We have viewed
clergy as "closer to God," therefore set apart from laity.
Phenomenologically speaking, this is the common perception of things. The clergy's authority of office, symbolized by special clothing, enhances the perception.
These perceptions, however, are the result of historical
developments and have no warrant, as far as I can tell,
from the perspective of a biblical theology of ministry.
Clergy are no more bearers of the sacred than are laity,
but they are no less either. Rather, as will be discussed in
somewhat greater detail in chapter 8, clergy have a particular representative role in the gathered community as
a symbol or reminder of the gift of holiness in which the
whole people of God share and which they are to
represent.

Recall my earlier family analogy. As I indicated, my
family was a center of my belonging that, my mother
hoped, would shape my values and inform my behavior
when I was away at college. My parents, especially my
father, came to symbolize the family's values, which I, no
less than he or other family members, was to represent.
He was no different from me in that respect; rather, he
simply modeled what I also was to be—and this gave

him a certain moral authority from my perspective. Similarly, the clergy's special symbolic role as a reminder of the gift of holiness to all of God's people constitutes one basis of their authority, as we have seen, but *it does not make clergy more holy than any other Christian.* As Martin Luther expressed it, all Christians are priests, called to be "little Christs" to their neighbors.

This calling, plus the competence to discern the relation of the gospel to their diverse ministry settings which enlivens their calling to be "little Christs," are the bases for the laity's authority to be in ministry. While these bases bear formal similarity to the bases for clergy authority, they differ in content and expression as they reflect the particular roles of laity and clergy in the economy of the church's ministry: The clergy's role is primarily, but not exclusively, in the gathered community; the laity's role is primarily, but not exclusively, in the church's scattered life. Each, however, is exercising authority in community and for the sake of community in ways that mutually support each other.

Gaining clarity about the commonalities and differences in lay and ordained ministry can be a profitable experience. I have often asked clergy and laity to answer, in separate groups, several questions about their own and the other's authority. Clergy answer the following questions: (1) How do I understand my authority as an ordained minister? (2) How do I think laity in the congregation understand my authority as an ordained minister? (3) How do I understand the laity's authority as ministers? (4) How do the laity understand their own authority for ministry? Laity answer the same questions, rephrased as follows: (1) How do I understand my authority for ministry as a layperson? (2) How do I think my pastor understands my authority for ministry? (3) How do I understand my pastor's authority for ministry? (4) How does my pastor understand her or his authority for ministry? When they have answered the questions, they share their results with each other, noting similarities and differences, blocking factors, and ways that they might mutually help each other to share ministry more effectively.

STRONG LEADERSHIP AND SYMMETRY

Let me conclude with a final assumption: Shared ministry and symmetrical, interdependent relationships between clergy and laity are not incompatible with strong leadership.

One of the greatest mistakes of the shared ministry emphasis is to assume that shared ministry and strong pastoral and lay leadership are contradictory. In a summary of a number of sociological studies of churches undertaken in the 1920s and '30s, H. Paul Douglass and Edmund deS. Brunner (1935, 254) concluded that most churches were heavily determined by the fortunes of their external environment: "As goes the neighborhood so goes the church." They also concluded that the most distinctive characteristic of those churches that had "risen above their environments and succeeded where most others had failed" (1935, 254) was exceptional leadership. More recently, the authors of a study of factors that help affluent congregations transcend the class interests of their members and become involved in social ministries concluded that

> The crucial factor in their involvement seems to be strong, prophetic leadership. When pastors clearly articulate that "you shall love the Lord with all your heart and soul and mind, and your neighbor as yourself" . . . , and when pastors and lay leaders are perceived as effective, responsible, and even visionary, affluent churches and their members become significantly more involved in the social problems of our times (Mock, Davidson, and Johnson 1991, 101).

My own experience in participating in and studying congregations, both small and large, has confirmed these generalizations. Strong leadership is essential for congregational vitality, but strong leadership need not be exercised at the expense of shared ministry.

One key to such leadership is the recognition that power in the church is not what game theorists call a "zero-sum" game. In a zero-sum situation, one assumes that power is a finite commodity. Whatever power I share with you diminishes my own power by that much. Thus, I jealously hoard my supply and keep you dependent on me. And you respond in a similar fashion. If I give to you, I do so paternalistically, still keeping you in the dependent relationship. Power in the church, however, need not be a zero-sum relationship. Paul understood that all members of the body of Christ share in the power of the Spirit that animates it. All have differing gifts of power (charisms), which are for the good of the whole. The secret of exercising power is not to hoard one's power or use it paternalistically but to learn together to honor each other's gifts and use one's own gift to strengthen and support the other.

Because power is not limited, a pastor who believes in shared ministry can be a strong leader without being authoritarian and paternalistic, without keeping laity in a dependent and secondary role. Rather, such pastors will acknowledge the laity's gifts and wisdom and be sure that they have the needed resources and support to exercise them. One need not be a nondirective, laissez-faire facilitator—a very wimpish image of ministry—in order to share ministry. Rather, the pastor will use his or her training and gifts of discernment to help individuals or the congregation as a whole examine the issues and options open to them in particular situations in light of who they are (memory) and why they are (hope) as Christians. Moreover, he or she will encourage, support, and inspire members to use their gifts for ministry to act on their insight and vision. David McClelland (1975, 262), in a study of power and leadership, sums up this kind of exercise of power as follows: "The positive . . .

face of power is characterized by a concern for group goals, for finding those goals that will move men [and women], for helping the group to formulate them, for taking initiative in providing means of achieving them, and for giving group members the feeling of competence they need to work hard for them."

While in no way do I claim that these five assumptions form an adequate ecclesiology, they provide a basis for the reinterpretation of authority and leadership that follows. They point to the story by which the church's practice, including its authority and leadership, is judged and shaped. Furthermore, they imply authority relationships that are relatively symmetrical but that nevertheless honor the distinctive roles of clergy and laity within the economy of the body of Christ.

5

THE CENTRAL TASKS
OF LEADERSHIP
IN THE CHURCH

"Ministry is connected with a special concern
for the preservation of the Christian identity
of the community in constantly changing
circumstances."
—Edward Schillebeeckx

The focus of this chapter is on core tasks of leadership in the church.[1] If one wishes to reconceive or reclaim his or her authority for leadership in the church, then it is important to be clear about the tasks that leaders are called to perform. My aim is to provide a description of these core tasks in which leaders engage as "reflective practitioners," a key concept to which we will return in subsequent chapters.

THE PRIMARY TASK:
ENSURING CHRISTIAN IDENTITY

In the last chapter, the church was described in contextual terms as a continuing incarnation of the Word in forms and expressions appropriate to different times,

97

places, and circumstances. This clearly does not imply sameness. As Karl Barth (1962, 739) once wrote: "There has never been anywhere . . . an intrinsically sacred sociology [of the church]." But neither is this to say that anything goes. The church's identity as the body of Christ precludes this. Ministry, both ordained and lay, is therefore "connected with a special concern for the preservation of the Christian identity of the community under constantly changing circumstances," to use Edward Schillebeeckx's succinct and helpful way of describing the primary task of leadership in the church. I prefer the word "ensuring" Christian identity rather than "preserving" it. It is more dynamic and suggests the church's *becoming* as well as its present *being* as the body of Christ. In any case, the primary task is ensuring the church's Christian identity in ways appropriate to different and changing contexts.

In a subsequent chapter, I emphasize the importance of taking seriously the culture and identity of particular local congregations as one leads reflectively. One must learn to "read" a congregation's particular culture, respect it, and lead from within it. In doing this, however, the *primary* task of leaders, ordained and lay, remains that of ensuring the congregation's identity as the body of Christ in ways that are appropriate to its particular culture and context. Insofar as a congregation is faithful to its calling to be the church, its particular identity must also give expression to its Christian identity.

Facets of the Core Task

In an important work on leadership, Philip Selznick (1957) used a three-fold description of the leader's task: defining the organization's mission and role, embodying that purpose in its organizational life, and helping the organization and its members give expression to their distinctive values in the face of threats from without and within. These three aspects of leadership, when applied to the church, indicate different dimensions of the primary task of ensuring the church's Christian identity. They can also be recast in ways that parallel the functional categories used to describe the church in the previous chapter: meaning, belonging, and empowerment. Using these categories, we can construe the leadership task in a similar way: as *meaning interpretation*, which includes articulating the church's primary mission as the body of Christ; *community formation*, building organizational structures and relationships that express the church's Christian identity; and *supporting the congregation's public ministry*, helping the church and its members to live as Christ's body in the world.

The three functions are interrelated ways of describing the single task of ensuring Christian identity. It is helpful to think of them as like facets of a cut diamond. There is but one stone, but it has different sides from which it can be viewed. While each facet reflects a peculiar angle on the one stone, it is not separable from the whole. It participates in it fully. Similarly, each of the three leadership functions provides a different but interdependent angle on the one core task of ministry. We can consider them separately, but in the life of the congregation they cannot be pulled apart.

These ways of characterizing leadership, especially clergy leadership, are important because they help to make new connections and see new possibilities that traditional role descriptions—which often appear to be discrete, unrelated tasks—may obscure. I shall describe each of the three facets and then present an extended example that helps to illustrate their meaning and interdependence.

MEANING INTERPRETATION

First, there is the clergy's function as *interpreter of meaning*. Much of what a pastor does in specific pastoral roles—preaching, designing and leading the liturgy, teaching, counseling, and organizational leadership—is aimed at assisting the congregation and its members to reflect on and interpret their life, individually and corporately, in light of God's purposes in Jesus Christ.

As individuals we face hopes, fears, disappointments, moral dilemmas, life changes, and life crises that challenge us with questions of meaning, often raising the issue of the ultimate meaningfulness of life. Transition points—childbirth, puberty, marriage, divorce, retirement, death—are particularly challenging moments that threaten to rip the fabric of meaning by introducing new and often unanticipated experiences.

Congregations also experience crises of meaning: decisions about the future, conflicts over particular programs, dilemmas over how to spend limited resources, interpersonal or intergroup conflicts, and many other such issues that call for reflection, interpretation, and decision.

The pastoral task is that of standing with individuals or the congregation as a corporate body in these experiences, helping them to face them and to give meaning to them in light of the gospel. The pastor helps members to reflect on these experiences, framing or reframing them in terms of the gospel and exploring responses to them in ways that express their Christian identity. Expressed slightly differently, the task is to break open the symbols of the tradition in such a way that they illumine the concrete and sometimes threatening issues of life, personal and social, in fresh and helpful ways.

The apostle Paul provides an example. For the early Christian community, Jesus' death on the cross was a radically disturbing experience. It created what social psychologists (e.g., Festinger 1957) call cognitive dissonance, a crisis of meaning that arises when one's expectations or beliefs are challenged by objective events or by other beliefs that appear to be contradictory. Paul's reinterpretation (reframing) of the cross as the foolishness and weakness of God, which is wiser and more powerful than that of the world (1 Cor. 1:25) and his use of the cross-resurrection theme as central symbols of Christians' experience are powerful examples of meaning interpretation. They enabled the early Christians to *celebrate* the foolishness of the cross and reframe their own life experiences in terms of Jesus' death and resurrection in ways that energized them for mission.[2]

Today we face a genuine difficulty: Many people find the teachings and symbols of faith opaque, out-of-touch with their experiences. They are like the young boy away at boarding school who wrote home after his first visit to the school's chapel: "It has lovely stained glass windows with pictures of people who were famous in God's time." Sometimes we seem to venerate the teachings and symbols of faith because they were important in "God's time," but it is often difficult to discern their meaning for "real time" here and now. As Presbyterian pastor Wallace Alston (1970) expressed it pungently, "the Christian community has allowed its language of faith to die without benefit of resurrection."

There are times when those of us who are clergy also find such discernment difficult. In Thomas Keneally's novel *Three Cheers for the Paraclete* (1968, 119–120), a priest wonders if the words of the sermons, the prayers, and the liturgy are not "shrines vacated by the deity." Was the fault in him, or "was the shrine too old, too far gone, too long outgrown by whatever God it once held?" Keneally's priest does not answer his question directly; rather, he does so indirectly as he struggles, against those who would perpetuate orthodox formulae for orthodoxy's sake, to understand the old symbols in fresh ways that connect with the here and now. That is a primary, albeit exceedingly difficult, task of clergy in the exercise of their authority. In the face of their own struggles with the meaning and relevance of the tradition, clergy will not speak with authority if they simply mouth the words of tradition, even if they mouth them loudly— in the manner of the preacher whose marginal sermon

notes reminded him, "Weak point. Shout like hell!" The
need, as Alston (1970, 4) put it,

> is for ministers who are willing to stay in a conflict-
> ridden local parish and to struggle for a vital lan-
> guage of faith that is both faithful to the tradition of
> the Church and historical for the contemporary mo-
> ment. We need ministers, in other words, who are
> willing to shun the temptation to be amateur psy-
> chiatrists or amateur sociologists and dare to do
> what they were trained and ordained to do, namely,
> to be theologians in the context of a local commu-
> nity of faith.

We have gone through a period of de-emphasis on
the pastor's role as meaning interpreter or theologian in
the congregation. Theological educators complain that
students are electing practical courses in the curriculum
and neglecting foundational courses that undergird the
practice. At the same time, some seminaries have contributed to the de-emphasis on meaning interpretation by
making courses in homiletics optional. Moreover, recent
accents in clergy continuing education seem to have been
more often on issues of organizational development and
conflict management than on the clergy's interpretive
roles, including developing the capacity to think theologically about parish management.

Meanwhile, laity continue to send signals about
their longing for help in discerning the meaning of the
faith for their lives. In parish survey after survey, parishioners express their greatest hope (and dissatisfaction
from unfulfilled hopes) that their church will assist them
in "deepening their spiritual life."[3] In a recent national
survey, Catholic and Protestant parish lay leaders expressed similar disappointment with their current clergy
leadership on the same issue (Hoge, Carroll, and Scheets
1989). The phrase "deepening their spiritual life" may
mean a number of things, but at heart it conveys an ex-

pectation by laity that their pastor will help them to connect their own stories, personal and parish, to the stories
and symbols of the Christian faith in a way that gives
meaning and direction to their lives. In other words, they
want clergy who will be the kind of theologians in the
congregation that Alston describes.

In the worship services of the church that our family
attends, we symbolize this expectation by the practice,
derived from early New England church life, of having a
layperson take the Bible from the communion table to
the pulpit and present it to the pastor at the time for the
lessons and sermon. Following the sermon, the pastor
returns the Bible to the congregation, putting it back on
the table. In this act, we symbolize our conviction that
we live under the authority of the Word, and we ask the
pastor to interpret that Word—break open the tradition
as the bread is broken in the Eucharist—in such a way
that it helps us to make sense of our experiences. Returning it to us reminds us of our responsibility to live out of
that Word as we scatter from the worship service to the
various settings where we are called to be in ministry.
Neither pastor nor congregation always succeeds in living up to the expectations of the ritual act. Nonetheless,
it is a potent reminder, Sunday after Sunday, of what we
expect of each other.

While meaning interpretation sounds as if it were
primarily a verbal, cognitive enterprise, it is considerably
more. Much in our lives occurs at a nondiscursive level—
things that we can feel, see, smell, hear, and do, but that
we find difficult, if not impossible, to put into words or
concepts. Anna Pavlova is said to have responded to a
questioner who asked "What do you say when you
dance?": "If I could tell you, I wouldn't dance." Reflecting on Pavlova's comment, Orrin Klapp (1969, 19–20)
refers to this and other nondiscursive modes of communication as "mystique." It is the whole meaning that a
person gets without being able to describe it verbally or
conceptually. Much of the meaning interpretation in

which the church engages has this nondiscursive character. Through the liturgy, in music, in the sacraments, in
symbols of the worship space, in priorities symbolized in
the church budget, in the coffee and donuts of the fellowship hour, in a silent presence with a family at a time
of bereavement, we communicate meanings that we cannot always put into words.

In acting as interpreter, the pastor exercises what I
called in chapter 2 *cultural* (as distinct from *social*) authority. The aim is not to determine or control the way
that others think or behave. Rather, the pastor's concern
is to influence the others' definitions of reality. She or he
gives them language, symbols, rituals, and stories and
helps them deal with their experiences of cognitive dissonance and make connections between these resources
and their experiences. The language, symbols, rituals,
and stories of faith become their stories, and their experiences are opened up with new possibilities and new
hope.

COMMUNITY FORMATION

The church is not only a place that helps us to give
meaning to our lives. As stated earlier, it is also a community of belonging in which individuals are called out
of their loneliness and isolation into caring, supportive
relationships with others who share a commitment to Jesus Christ. It is a community where members are nurtured in the virtues of Christian life. And it is through the
quality of its community life that the church bears witness to the meaning of justice and reconciliation as marks
of God's coming reign that is both present now and yet
to come. This requires a second leadership task: *community formation*, helping to shape the congregation as a
community of belonging. More specifically, it is to help
shape it in ways that embody its identity as the body of
Christ.

A close relationship exists between this task and

meaning interpretation. Each task reinforces the other in the service of ensuring Christian identity. Telling the gospel story helps to define the character and contours of Christian community. Participation in a community that offers fellowship, expresses caring and support, and seeks justice in the relationships of its members is an eloquent example in action of the meaning of the gospel story. Conversely, even the most persuasive telling of the gospel story will have difficulty overcoming the negative witness of a mean-spirited, unjust community.

Building vital Christian community is essential to maintaining Christian identity in yet another way. Primary communities such as the church are examples of what Peter Berger and Thomas Luckmann (1967) have called "plausibility structures." Such communities sustain the plausibility or believability of a particular understanding of reality through conversation and through various symbolic and ritual expressions. As Berger (1967, 46–47) has written, "*all* religious traditions, irrespective of their several 'ecclesiologies' or lack of same, require specific communities for their continuing plausibility." This, he suggests, is one general meaning of the maxim "Outside the church there is no salvation." When there are weak plausibility structures so also "the Christian world begins to totter and its reality ceases to impose itself [to the individual] as self-evident truth. . . . The firmer the plausibility structure is, the firmer will be the world that is 'based' upon it." Put another way, the more powerful the experience of belonging to a congregation, the more plausible and vital will be its interpretation of the Christian story.

For all these reasons, the belonging dimension of the church is not an option. Community formation is a primary leadership task, with pastors working to form and sustain the relationships and structures of the gathered community and helping it maintain its identity as the body of Christ. As the author of Ephesians expressed it, the aim is "building up the body of Christ, until we all attain to the unity of the faith and of the knowledge of the Son of God, . . . to the measure of the stature of the fullness of Christ" (Eph. 4:13).

One element of the clergy's community formation role is as celebrant of the sacraments, incorporating individuals into the family of God in baptism, bringing people together around the table in the Eucharist. There is an obvious overlap with the interpretative role just described, especially with some of its nondiscursive elements.

Biblical scholar Wayne Meeks (1983) demonstrates this connection, using the tools of sociology, in his fascinating analysis of Pauline congregations. Paul's interpretation of baptism and Eucharist created powerful symbolic means of community formation as well as meaning interpretation in the face of cognitive dissonance. Those who were converts to the churches were a disparate group: people of means (especially wealthy women), artisans, tradesmen, masters, and slaves. If they shared anything in common, it was discrepant statuses, statuses that were partly valued, partly devalued in the social world of the first century. Their rituals, especially baptism and Eucharist, provided powerful, mostly nonverbal symbols of participation in a new reality and a new community. Entrants into the community died to the old statuses that defined them in society and were raised to a new sense of personhood in fellowship with Christ and with each other. They participated in a new interpretation of their lives and a new community. Baptism symbolized this nonverbally as new entrants experienced the drama of being stripped of their old identity (often literally, by shedding their clothes) and cleansed of the past and raised to new relationship with Christ and one another. The Lord's Supper, with its sharing together in Christ's death and resurrection, incorporated them into a new community, promoted solidarity, and helped them define a distinctive Christian identity.

These sacraments continue to be central nondiscursive means for shaping Christian identity: baptism as the event that incorporates us into God's family and gives us our vocation to ministry as God's people; Eucharist as the continuing renewal of communion with Christ and one another in God's family and reminder that our Christian identity is expressed in a servant ministry of life broken and poured out for others. These and other liturgical actions are central to the clergy's role in community formation.

Community formation also requires theological and sociological insight into the nature and functioning of communities and the skills of a midwife in assisting it into being—the ability to understand congregations and their dynamics, managerial and administrative skills, skills in group relationships and conflict management, as well as political and persuasive skills. Its aim is a community life whose structures and processes are faithful to its identity as the body of Christ and also appropriate to the concrete situation in which the congregation finds itself—its size, its resources, its setting.

In spite of what was said earlier about the growing emphasis on organizational development and conflict management in clergy continuing education opportunities, neither clergy nor theological educators always view the managerial and administrative aspects of community building as particularly important or as having theological warrant. Samuel Blizzard's studies in the 1950s (Blizzard 1956) revealed that these more "mundane" tasks occupy at least half of a pastor's time in an average week. At the same time, the administrative and organizational roles are the least satisfying and least well legitimated from a normative perspective. Although Blizzard's findings are over three decades old, they appear still to be an accurate description of the situation.

In a recent study of doctor of ministry programs (Carroll and Wheeler 1987), almost 2,400 clergy from a broad spectrum of denominations were surveyed. When clergy were given descriptive paragraphs of various role images of parish ministry and were asked to rate each in terms of its appropriateness as a self-description, respondents overwhelmingly said that the "Minister of the Word/Teacher of the Congregation" image was most like them. This, of course, is another way of describing the meaning interpretation task. Three community building images—Celebrant/Liturgist, Enabler/Facilitator, and especially Parish Administrator—ranked considerably lower as self-descriptors.[4]

When H. Richard Niebuhr (1956) proposed "pastoral director" as an appropriate image of ordained ministry, critics faulted him for lending credence to what seemed to be a "big operator," management-oriented, nontheological view of ordained ministry—what Hough and Cobb (1985) refer to as the Manager model of ministry. "Pastoral director" may have suggested this, but it was clearly not what Niebuhr intended. Instead, he derived his image from the monastic tradition and intended by it leadership in community formation and maintenance. Such a role, as Niebuhr pointed out, not only continues to be of central importance to the church but has historic links with the early church's role of bishop (*episcopos*), who functioned as overseer of one or more congregations by presiding at the Eucharist and by giving pastoral guidance (including administration) to the gathered life of the community. The church continues to require such leadership as a means of ensuring its Christian identity under changing circumstances.

EMPOWERING PUBLIC MINISTRY

The third pastoral task reflects the role of the church as a community of empowerment. The aim is empowering members, individually and collectively, to live as the people of God in the world. A somewhat more awkward way of describing it is as managing the interface between the church's gathered and scattered life.

This pastoral task is analogous to a role that community development workers have created in Haiti. They train leaders whom they call "animateurs," men and women who learn group formation and mobilization techniques to help others in their groups respond constructively to their situations. Animateurs are trained to help their groups analyze their problems, explore solutions, and develop ways to implement them. As one author (Hollar 1988) described the goal: "The key is to 'animate groups to think and act for themselves, not to dictate decisions from outside.' " A similar role is required of clergy who become animateurs of their congregations with respect to their corporate and individual ministries beyond the walls of the church.

This is no simple or easy task. It has become increasingly difficult for Christians to speak with the language of faith or act in accord with their Christian identity in secular social settings. A secular society, such as the one in which we live, attempts to render public expressions of faith, either in language or behavior, as *mere* personal opinion at best and in bad taste at worst. It is, therefore, no mean task for clergy and laity to discover ways of asserting the power and relevance of their faith in contexts that generally exclude the relevance of religious speech and behavior. Sometimes this requires bold and explicit profession of one's faith and its implications. No other way seems defensible. At the same time, we are also called to accompany our witness with a willingness to remain in dialogue with other perspectives and a humility that prevents us from claiming a direct line to God. Such humility is especially important when there are so frequently honest disagreements as to what the will of God is in this or that situation. I once was asked by a fellow campus minister to accompany him and his attorney to a hearing where he had applied for a license to serve beer in an off-campus coffeehouse that was a part of his ministry. The director of a nearby funeral home had contested his application. The funeral director had brought his pastor in support of his position. The presiding officer confessed surprise and confusion: "I've frequently had reverends on one side of the table, but this is the first time I've had them on both sides!" One person's virtue is frequently at odds with another's. How much more is this true in such complex, difficult issues as abortion rights, efforts to redress past injustices through affirmative hiring, or attempts to achieve racial balance in school districts, to mention but a few.

Often, however, what is called for is adopting what Dietrich Bonhoeffer (1955, 84ff.) called a penultimate rather than ultimate attitude. This means foregoing speech or action that explicitly expresses one's ultimate faith convictions. It involves, instead, finding penultimate ways of living out of one's convictions, ways of speaking and acting that respect the everyday reality that we share with others in the situation who may not hold our ultimate convictions. It involves finding common ground with them on which to work for the common good: more humane, fair, or just solutions to issues at work, in the community, or in the nation. Bonhoeffer asks:

> Does one not in some cases, by remaining deliberately in the penultimate, perhaps point all the more genuinely to the ultimate, which God will speak in His own time? . . . Does not this mean that, over and over again, the penultimate will be what commends itself precisely for the sake of the ultimate, and that it will have to be done not with a heavy conscience but with a clear one?

One can argue that the role of empowerment really derives from the meaning interpretation and community formation roles. If the pastor's role as interpreter of meaning includes helping laity explore their calling in terms of concrete issues of family, work, or public life, then the pastor is already engaged in the empowering role. Similarly, if pastors are helping to form a commu-

nity in the church where individuals find healing, renewal, and support and are nurtured in the virtues of the
Christian life, they are also engaged in supporting the
public ministries of these persons.

Empowering public ministry warrants emphasis as a
distinctive task for two reasons. One is the ease in which
we come to subsume the meaning of church in terms of
its gathered life. Emphasizing the task of supporting public ministry focuses attention on the life of the people of
God in the world as the primary arena for ministry. Second, clergy too belong to the *laos*, God's people in the
world. In spite of the priority attention that clergy must
give to the gathered life of the church, they have vital
and important roles in the broader community, modeling
what it means to live as Christians in public life and acting as symbolic representatives of religion in public affairs. I do not advocate either the restriction of the clergy
role to the internal life of the church, a nineteenth-
century invention, or the view, so pervasive today, that
limits the congregation's role (clergy and laity) to the private sphere.

Several years ago two colleagues and I studied the
relation of religion to public life in Hartford, Connecticut
(McKinney, Roozen, and Carroll 1983; Roozen, McKinney, and Carroll 1984). A primary finding was the importance of pastoral leadership for shaping how a
congregation related to public life, whether this relationship was interpreted as winning converts, providing service, or engaging in social action. How pastors defined
and interpreted the congregation's role in public life, and
how they modeled that role in their own involvement in
the life of the community, were crucial to the congregation's orientation and involvement (or lack thereof) in
public life. Additionally, we found that community leaders tended to identify religion with religious professionals. Unless ministers, priests, or rabbis were themselves
visible in public affairs, religion itself was often viewed
as absent.

There are clearly problems with such a view from the perspective of shared ministry. It is laity who are daily inhabitants of the institutions of the public world and whose primary calling is to exercise their ministries in these institutions. Clergy, nevertheless, play a crucial role in this arena. Beyond their symbolic role as institutional representatives of religion, they need also to bring expertise to the church–social context interface. This includes the capacity to analyze community dynamics and public issues, an understanding of both the penultimate character of issues and their relation to the Christian story, and a willingness to engage with others (inside and outside the church) in reflection and action on the issues.

Putting It Together: An Example

Each of the three core tasks of ministry implies a repertoire of specific methods and skills for clergy in such roles as preaching, teaching, organizational management, social analysis, and so forth. The three share, nevertheless, at least one common requirement. Each requires the capacity to lead others in reflection: analyzing situations, seeing their relationship to the Christian story, and discerning options for responding to the situations in ways that give expression to Christian identity. This is a shorthand way of describing reflective leadership, which I will discuss at some length in the following chapters.

Before doing so, let me conclude the discussion of the three core tasks of ministry with an extended example. Earlier the three core tasks were described as similar to facets of a single stone—each distinct but also part of a whole. I further alluded to their interrelationship as each was discussed. The meanings associated with Christian identity help to give belonging a focus and a purpose. We do not belong for belonging's sake. We belong to the community of Jesus Christ. Belonging, in turn, provides the context—the plausibility structures—whereby the meanings are explored, rehearsed, and sustained in mutual conversation and ritual behavior. Both meaning and belonging are, in turn, essential for empowering the church's ministry in public life. And attempting to live out of a Christian identity in public life opens up new questions of meaning and makes us aware of our need of a supportive and sustaining community. Thinking of the three core tasks in this mutually interdependent way helps us to think holistically about the life and mission of the church and the roles of clergy and laity, as the example helps us to see.

COLCHESTER FEDERATED CHURCH

Colchester Federated Church[5] (United Church of Christ and American Baptist) is a congregation located in what until recently was a small Connecticut town that had not been affected much by urban growth. The church, which averaged about fifty persons at morning worship in the mid-1970s, consisted primarily of members who were farmers, clerical and production workers, and small-business people. They were faithful and loyal members but unaccustomed to thinking in new ways about their church's mission. By the 1980s, however, the town and congregation experienced a growth spurt with younger, more professionally educated workers moving in and joining the church. They brought new ideas and created a leaven for change. In 1980 the church called a new pastor, the Rev. Davida Foy Crabtree. Under her leadership, the church has grown in membership and member involvement. Average worship attendance in 1988 was approximately 150. More important, the church has also grown in the way it expresses its corporate life and mission.

When Crabtree came to the church, the pastor was committed to a vision of the ministry of the laity, drawn from the larger Christian tradition, that became the guiding image for much of her work in pastoral care and organizational leadership. While she found some laity in the congregation who affirmed this vision, it was not really shared by the majority of members, except perhaps in the perfunctory way that many Protestants express belief in the "priesthood of all believers." The vision was part of the congregation's broader Christian identity, but it was not an operational part of the local culture of the congregation, which tended to restrict ministry to the ordained leader.

Initially, she expressed her vision primarily in preaching and in teaching opportunities that she initiated, for example, an adult retreat ("Discovering Our Gifts") and a conference ("Beyond a Sunday Christianity"). During this time, the leadership also began a planning process—the congregation's first experience with formal planning—and the pastor entered a doctor of ministry program intent on making shared ministry the focus of her work.

A major breakthrough in developing greater ownership of the shared ministry emphasis came in 1986 with the recognition that retreats and conferences were familiar ways of working for college-educated, middle-class managers and professionals, but they were somewhat alien to less verbally skilled working-class people. Therefore, she formed a listening team of three laity (a machinist, an executive, and a data base analyst), who invited occupational groups to spend an evening talking about their work. The pastor served as a silent observer-recorder. The people—teachers, office workers, and production workers—were encouraged to talk about their satisfactions and frustrations, and they were asked a question that invariably stymied them: "Does it make any difference that you are a Christian on your job?" Despite the difficulty, feedback indicated that the experience was a positive one, and some wanted to go further.

A next step was the creation of a covenant group of twelve members, who spent ten months together considering issues of faith and work with both the pastor and a new associate pastor participating, symbolic of the importance that both clergy attached to the emphasis. Through various ways—Bible study, case studies of work situations, reading, and sharing work experiences—group members developed a capacity to think and talk about their faith and its relation to their work and other aspects of their lives, a new experience for most of them. For example, the somewhat esoteric biblical concepts of "principalities and powers" came alive for them as they explored the ways that institutional aspects of the work situation and church practice seem to have a life of their own and often seem to hold people in bondage. So too did the meaning of Christ as liberator—a central image of the pastor's theology—take on new importance. Members also experienced significant caring and support from others in the group. They encouraged and held each other accountable for the exercise of their ministries in daily life. Subsequently, other covenant groups were formed along the lines of the first one.

Various ways of including the broader congregation in the covenant groups' work were used, including additional conferences and retreats. With the groups' assistance, the pastors began to include a special vocation prayer in the Sunday worship. Members provided suggestions from their work experience to help shape the prayers. A different occupation was featured each week with a visual reminder of the work placed on the Communion table before the cross. A prayer was said for all in that occupation. For example, when electricians were the focus, coils of wire and some tools were placed in the table, and the following prayer was used:

> Creator God, You are the source of all Energy and Power. We bring before You this day those who work with the power of electricity, who seek to channel, transform and convert a dangerous energy into power for good. Guard them and keep them safe. Give them patience with tracking problems to their source, and caution in their work. And grant

them a sense of ministry in their making our lives
safe, in their striving for excellence, in their dealings
with people In the name of Jesus, Amen (Crabtree
1989, 6).

Meanwhile, as part of a course assignment, the pastor "shadowed" several members of her congregation at
their work; that is, she shared a workday with them,
observing their on-the-job experiences. She found that
this opened significant new opportunities for pastoral
care, and now she regularly meets parishioners for lunch
in their work settings.

As the emphasis on ministry in the workplace progressed, the pastor and some of her leaders became
aware of a deeper issue that had to be addressed if it
were to take hold in a significant and lasting way: The
structure of the congregation itself had to be addressed.
As presently organized, the congregation is what she
calls a "come" structure: It is concerned primarily with
bringing members to the church building to participate in
and support its gathered life. It is not a "go out" structure
that also supports and encourages ministry in the
church's scattered life. As she sees it (Crabtree 1988, 18),
"If a congregation is going to be serious about supporting
its members in discerning and living out their ministries,
it must be prepared to incarnate that support in the sys-
tems of its life." To initiate this kind of reflection, she
developed a group of questions for each board and committee, inviting them to consider how their work might
be recast to empower the ministry of the laity both
within the congregation and, especially, beyond it. She
began to shape the outlines of what she called a "management system" to structure the church so that it would
more effectively empower lay ministry. Sharing this with
the diaconate, reinforced by discussions with them on
the meaning of ministry, led to the creation of a special
short-term task force to develop a plan for restructuring
the congregation as a "go out" structure under the diaco-

nate's leadership. That process is currently underway with indications that a growing number of lay leaders and members have come to share their pastor's vision. At the same time, they are sensitive to those members who have not yet caught the vision and who look to the church with more traditional expectations. They are concerned that these people not feel neglected or excluded from the church's ministry.

This is an exciting and encouraging story, only a part of which I have been able to tell here. It is also an ongoing story. A real test will come in the congregation's ability to sustain and grow in its emphasis on shared ministry, with or without its current pastor. My major reason for telling the story, however, is as a clear example of the interrelationship and interdependence of the three core tasks of ministry.

The pastor's initial focus was on the third task, encouraging and supporting the laity's public ministry, especially in their work life. That was reinforced by preaching and teaching—meaning interpretation—in which she tried to help members understand their vocation to ministry. Later, too, the members' vocation to ministry became part of the liturgy and symbols in the vocation prayers. Had she stopped with the interpretive task, however, it is unlikely that her vision would have taken hold in the consciousness of the members. In addition to the worship services, the covenant group experience provided an important "plausibility structure" and center for belonging where faith and everyday experience could be talked about frankly in a supportive, caring environment. The groups also took on the character of accountability as well as plausibility structures, where people not only talk about their convictions but hold one another accountable for living by them. Even more was needed, however, if the vision was to take shape and become incarnate as part of the congregation's identity and character: It had to became part of the institutional fabric, thus the emphasis on the management system that is still underway in the church. How that restructuring takes shape and whether it can overcome years of doing things "the way we've always done them" remains to be seen. It is, however, a crucial aspect of community building that leaders must undertake if the congregation is to embody its vision.

I wish to emphasize that I do not intend this as an example that other congregations should attempt to duplicate. For many congregations the particular expression of their vision may be different, dictated by the way they understand their calling to live out a Christian identity in their distinctive culture and context. Yet however they give concrete expression to their vision of what it means for them to be Christ's body, it will need to be interpreted in preaching and teaching and celebrated liturgically so that members can understand their own experiences and stories and their congregation's story in its light. It must also be sustained in a community where it becomes real through conversation, sharing, and support and where the community is structured in such a way to incarnate the vision. And members need support and a sense of accountability to live out of the vision, individually and corporately, in the church's scattered life. These things will not happen without strong leadership, especially that of clergy who function as meaning interpreters, community builders, and enablers of public ministry. I use the term "reflective leadership" to characterize the kind of leadership that can function authoritatively in these roles.

6

LEADING WITH AUTHORITY: THE DYNAMICS OF REFLECTIVE LEADERSHIP

> Managers are not confronted with problems that are independent of each other, but with dynamic situations that consist of complex systems of changing problems that interact with each other. I call such situations *messes*. Problems are abstractions extracted from messes by analysis. . . . Managers do not solve problems: they manage messes.
>
> —Russell Ackoff

As clergy lead their congregations in confronting questions of meaning, engage in community building, and enable public ministry, they confront various levels of complexity. Some issues are routine. They evoke little difficulty or controversy. They can usually be addressed by methods and techniques of practice that have worked in the past. These routine, nonproblematic situations are not my concern here. Rather, the focus is on the more complex, nonroutine issues: those that challenge the leadership capacities of clergy and laity and raise questions of authority. While we may thank God for the small, routine problems, more often than not we are faced, in Russell Ackoff's words, with "messes," complex and dynamic sets of problems that are often ill defined, unstructured, and open ended. Whether the issue is one of a meaningful pastoral response following the accidental death of a teenager, wrestling with a difficult sermon text, establishing budget priorities, dealing with a staff conflict, or taking a stance on a controversial social problem—to name just a few examples—such issues rarely lend themselves to routine solutions or to textbook formulae. Furthermore, rarely is there agreement as to *the* appropriate way to respond. All this simply acknowledges what one of my clergy heroes, Carlyle Marney, once said with his typical pungency: "Life never did lie down and behave for long, for anybody" (Kratt 1979, 89).

The challenge for the people of God, individually and corporately, is to find the resources to make sense of and respond to the particular messes that they face. In particular, the challenge is finding resources to respond in ways that honor their Christian identity, even when doing so involves risking being wrong or contradicting other interests. The special challenge for clergy—as interpreters of meaning, community builders, and enablers of public ministry—is to exercise their leadership authority so that individuals and congregations are helped to respond in ways that are Christianly apt.

A way of meeting this special challenge is the subject of this chapter and the following two. The chapters build on the general perspective on authority in the church developed in chapter 2. Recall especially the two penultimate bases of clergy authority: being a representative of the sacred and having a distinctive expertise. Recall also the distinction between personal and institutional (office) authority. I noted too that personal authority has grown in significance and seems likely to continue to do so. I want to look anew at these two penultimate bases and propose a way of thinking about them that is appropriate to the challenges that clergy face in leading in the midst of "messes." I consider the kind of expertise that is needed in this and the following chapter. Such expertise may be certified in ordination (authority of office), but it must be demonstrated in practice (personal authority). In the final chapter, I consider how the needed expertise is grounded in the clergy's relation to the sacred.

A META-METHOD FOR MINISTRY

What kind of expertise is needed by pastors if they are to function with authority? The way we have organized our seminary curriculum indicates that we believe that clergy expertise involves a working knowledge of the Bible, theology, the history of the church, ethics, and various theories and techniques of leadership and group life appropriate to the different roles of ordained ministry and the church. We master these subjects in seminary so that we can bring them to bear constructively on the issues of meaning, belonging, and empowerment that we encounter in the congregation or other ministry setting. This is what it means to function with authority as a professional. Would that it were as simple as this!

Learning the biblical story, the history of the church, theology, and the theories and techniques of ministry is one thing. Having the ability to use these resources creatively and constructively in practice, even to invent new resources, is quite another—especially as one confronts the complex "messes" of practice with which the modern world confronts us! The expertise that gives clergy their authority is the combination of specialized knowledge *and* the ability to draw on it reflectively in the midst of practice. Both are essential. What this implies is a kind of overarching method for ministry—"meta-method" is more accurate—that enables clergy to draw on their knowledge in the multiple roles and changing contexts in which a pastor functions. I use the term *meta-method* to suggest a method that applies broadly to clergy practice, that informs the more specific methods and techniques connected to particular clergy roles—for example, preaching, pastoral counseling, and conflict management. In what follows I want to introduce such a meta-method. Drawing on recent work by Donald Schön (1983, 1987), this meta-method may be referred to as "reflective leadership." I mean by it the capacity, in the midst of the practice of ministry, to lead the church to act in ways that are faithful to the gospel and appropriate within the situation. To lead reflectively involves a kind of hermeneutic of practice. It entails the capacity to "read" situations, and, in the midst of them, draw on resources of knowledge, experience, and skills—often by inventing new ones—to construct faithful and appropriate responses. It means also having an identity and personal style that inspire trust and confidence among those with whom one shares ministry.* Clergy who function as reflective leaders function with authority—not in a top-down, asymmetrical fashion but in partnership with laity.

Before examining the dynamics of reflective leadership in more detail, let me first explain why I believe such a meta-method is essential.

One of the continuing complaints about theological education is that it is not related to the "real world" of clergy practice. The theology and theories taught in the seminary seem remote from the concrete situations of clergy practice. Recent graduates often complain that they find it difficult to relate what they learned in the classroom to the concrete issues of ministry with which the parish confronts them. A crude way of expressing this complaint is that "All those theories don't preach!" A more elegant way of expressing it is Francis Bacon's description of philosophers: "[They] make imaginary laws for imaginary commonwealths; and their discourses

---

*I deal with this latter aspect of reflective leadership in chapter 7.

are as the stars, which give little light because they are so high" (quoted by Wood 1985, 64f.).

Denominational executives and laity sometimes voice similar complaints about clergy, often about recent seminary graduates. "They have a lot of knowledge *about* ministry, but not much knowledge of *how* to minister. They're great at theorizing about the church and its mission but deficient in knowing how to get things done." Conversely, many seminary faculty shake their heads in dismay when they have occasion to witness the practice of their graduates. "Where did we go wrong? Did we not give them a better grounding in Bible and theology than they exhibit in their various pastoral roles? They seem to have lost their vision and the capacity to think theologically about ministry." Laity express similar complaints. As in one of the vignettes of clergy in chapter 1, laity sometimes express admiration for the ministry skills of their pastor: ability to lead groups, knowledge of the latest stewardship or church growth strategies, public speaking skills, and so forth. But they may also feel that something is lacking which is hard for them to define: Their pastor "lacks spiritual depth." He or she doesn't seem to be able to help them understand the relationship of the gospel to issues and crises that arise in the course of their lives. He or she doesn't help them develop a compelling vision of the purpose of their church that puts budgets and new member recruitment and a multitude of church programs and activities in a larger, challenging perspective.

These various complaints seem contradictory: one bemoaning a lack of practical competence, the others complaining about the lack of evidence that theological knowledge and thinking informs ministry practice. While the complaints represent different points of view, they actually address different sides of a common problem: the relation between theory and practice. One group complains that the knowledge gained in seminary, including biblical and historical studies, theology and ethics, and theories about various aspects of practice, are remote from if not irrelevant to the actual tasks of ministry. The other complaint—that pastors reveal a lack of theological insight about ministry practice—is simply the other side of the theory-practice issue. While one might think that this is a problem that will be overcome as clergy gain experience in their practice and find ways of applying the theories learned in seminary, this is often wishful thinking. Many fail to do so ever, and they muddle through their careers, grasping at various straws of techniques that promise a quick fix. What is lacking is the capacity for reflective leadership. To use a biblical metaphor, they lack both the capacity to envision what bodily form a collection of dry bones might take and the ability to help them get connected so that the Spirit can breathe new life into them. Lacking these abilities, they also lack authority based on expertise in ministry practice.

REFLECTIVE LEADERSHIP: A CLOSER LOOK

In a recent work on theological education, Charles Wood (1985) uses two visual metaphors, *vision* and *discernment*, to discuss the task of theological education. He draws on an image from the Greek poet Archilocus: "The fox knows many things, but the hedgehog knows one big thing" (p. 68). The hedgehog is a metaphor for the capacity to develop a coherent vision of things; the fox represents the capacity to see the concrete thing in all its complexity. Some, as Wood notes, have suggested that these are opposing abilities; one is either a fox or a hedgehog, but not both. Wood, however, believes that it is possible for a person to be both, to have "a coherent understanding of the Christian witness as a whole" [vision], and "to grasp and assess the character of a particular instance of Christian witness [discernment]" (Wood 1985, 69; 73). He believes that a core task of theological education is to help students develop both capacities. While Wood's focus is on what vision and discernment

mean in the structure and practice of theological education, his metaphors of vision and discernment are helpful ways of describing the core elements of reflective
leadership. Without vision, one will be unlikely to lead a
congregation beyond the status quo. But without discernment, without an accurate picture of the reality of the
particular instance of practice, vision will more likely foster cynicism than creativity.

The critical question for reflective leaders is how to
get vision and discernment together as they go about their
meaning defining, community building and empowering
tasks. How can one's vision of Christian existence become
flesh compellingly in ways that are appropriate to particular situations and places? Is it a matter of developing theories that are more closely tied to the demands of practice?
Is it a matter of learning better techniques for applying
theory to practice? Or is neither of these sufficient?

In thinking about these matters, the work of Donald
Schön is especially provocative and helpful. Schön is
Professor of Urban Studies and Education at the Massachusetts Institute of Technology. In two recent books
(Schön 1983, 1987), he has extended John Dewey's earlier ideas about "reflective thinking" (Dewey 1933) and
applied them to professional practice. In doing so, Schön
developed the idea of "reflective practice" as both a critique of prevailing assumptions about how theory relates
to professional practice and as a constructive statement
about the nature of practice. His perspective, which I examine in some detail, has struck a responsive chord
among theological educators.[1] First, I will sketch some of
Schön's key insights about reflective practice. Then I will
use them to interpret two cases of ministry practice.

THE REFLECTIVE PRACTITIONER

From extensive observation of practicing professionals, Schön has become aware of a serious fallacy in the
usual assumption made about the theory-practice rela-

tionship in professional practice. This assumption, a form of "technical rationality," holds that there is a standard body of scientifically derived theory and a set of skills that one learns in professional schools. As professionals confront problems of practice, they select from their theories and techniques the ones that they can apply in practice for the achievement of some unambiguous end. For the doctor, the end is health; for the lawyer, successful litigation; for the business manager, profit (Schön 1987, 33).

When the technical rationality model is applied to the clergy professional, it takes the familiar theory-to-practice form: We go to seminary to learn basic knowledge that reflects rigorous scholarship based on the norms of the academy—for example, knowledge of the Bible and principles of biblical criticism, church history, theology and ethics, and theories of ministry practice. We also learn methods and skills for applying the theories—for example, techniques of preaching, counseling, or church growth. And, if we are lucky, we develop a vision of the end or goal of ministry, whether it be defined in terms of personal salvation or liberation of the oppressed. On graduation, we should then able to realize our ministry goal by applying the theory and techniques to the concrete issues that we face in the parish or other ministry setting, with the acknowledgment that formal continuing education will be needed to fill lacunae in our basic seminary preparation and update us with new developments in theories and skills for practice. Our authority lies in the expertise that we have—that laity do not have—in applying theology and theories to achieve ministry goals.

One can argue that the theories learned in seminary are less scientific than those, for example, of medicine. The precise meaning of the goal of ministry practice—salvation or liberation, for example—may also be more difficult to define than is the case for health. Thus, too, the means that clergy apply in a given instance of practice may be more open to debate. In spite of these differences, we often make the assumption of a theory-to-practice application for clergy practice that generally approximates the technical rationality model. Indeed, much of the emphasis on the professionalization of ministry and theological education that began in the late nineteenth century tried to match theological education more closely with the demands of ministry practice so that both would be more scientific—matching means to ends in a more technically rational manner.[2] H. Paul Douglass, an important early twentieth-century sociologist of church life, called for the development of "scientific churchmanship," so that one could apply scientifically determined standards to problems churches and pastors face (Douglass 1926, 39). He often despaired, however, that this would actually happen. Other professions underwent similar efforts to make them more scientific, more technically rational, during the same period.

Schön's work radically questions this model of professional education and practice and the assumptions about professional authority based on it. He does not deny the importance of values and norms that professions and professional schools seek to inculcate in their members. These are essential in guiding behavior and setting boundaries on appropriate professional practice. Nor does Schön deny the importance of bodies of professional knowledge—theories and techniques—that must be learned. Instead, he challenges the assumption that either the values and norms—vision elements, in my terms—or the theories and techniques can be applied to concrete instances of practice in a technically rational fashion.

He begins, rather, by assuming that many, if not most, of the problems of practice that professionals face are nonroutine, marked by uncertainty, instability, uniqueness, and value conflict over ends and appropriate means. Such situations defy technically rational assumptions of practice. There is no one best way to apply one's theories, nor is there often clarity about the end(s) of specific situations of practice. Schön agrees with Ackoff's observation that much of the professional's time is spent "managing messes" that do not allow for stable, textbook solutions. In such situations, the ends as well as the means of practice are often unclear and only emerge as the professional engages in a reflective conversation with the situation.

The contextual perspective on the church put forward earlier (chapter 4), where clergy and laity must struggle to discover what it means to live out their identity as the body of Christ in particular times and places, also makes clear the impossibility of textbook solutions to ministry practice. There is no one best way that can be applied in every ministry situation. Discovering how to respond involves a reflective act in which one incorporates a variety of resources and perspectives in an effort to be faithful to the church's calling. He or she recognizes that, although all things are partial, nonetheless what is done is in the nature of a parable, a pointer to the shape of Jesus' ministry.

From reflection on everyday life and especially from his observation of professionals in action, Schön proposes the model of reflective practice as a more helpful description of the way that competent professionals actually function. He also proposes an approach to professional education using the reflective practice model.

Excluding the most routine situations, Schön maintains that professionals engage in what he refers to as "reflection-in-action," a process involving a considerable amount of artistry and intuition on the professional's part. Theories are important, but they are only part of a complex way of knowing, often tacit, that takes place in the midst of acting. When competent professionals face nonroutine, complex problems, they typically treat them not as textbook cases but as unique situations, which they try to understand.

They begin by framing the problem and their role in

it in a way that is commensurate with their values and their initial reading of the circumstances surrounding the problem. That is, they give some initial definition to the problem by which they try to put the bits and pieces in perspective. They may ask themselves whether this is similar to other problems in their experience or in the theories and experiences of others. Is it like "this" or is it more like "that"? Much, however, of the knowing-in-action that they bring to the problem, including the initial framing of the issue, is what Schön (following Michael Polanyi [1958]) calls "tacit knowledge." It is knowledge that we draw on implicitly without intermediate reasoning, much the same as we do when we recognize the face of an acquaintance in a large crowd or when we learn to ride a bicycle.

Using both tacit and explicit knowledge, reflective practitioners may then try some ways of responding to the problem that their initial interpretation suggests; Schön calls these "frame experiments." Such experiments are the heart of reflective practice. They may be of several kinds: They may simply be *exploratory*, consisting of "probing, playful activity by which we get a feel for things," without any prediction or expectation that they will succeed. They succeed when they "lead to the discovery of something there" (Schön 1983, 145). There are also *move-testing* experiments, deliberate actions taken with an end in mind. They succeed when they produce the expected end and fail when they do not. In either case, however, they often produce other unintended consequences, which may be positive or negative. Finally, experiments may be *for the purpose of hypothesis testing*, trying to decide whether one course of action is more effective than another. Which will be the most effective way to meet my goals? This, or that?

As they reflect-in-action on what they are doing and attend to talkback from the situation, reflective practitioners may make one of several responses. They may continue with the course they have chosen, especially if it seems to be working. They may try other solutions and assess their implications for the problem. Or, they may reassess their original understanding of the problem, reframe the problem, and test it with another on-the-spot experiment. The framing-experimentation-reframing sequence continues until some resolution is found or until one decides that it is a presently intractable problem. The successes or failures of the process become part of the practitioner's experience and tacit knowledge and may provide exemplars for future situations of practice. Depending on the issue, this sequence of reflection-in-action may occur in a single encounter or over a more extended period of time.

Here is how Schön summarizes the process that he has observed:

> In each instance, the practitioner allows himself to experience surprise, puzzlement, or confusion in a situation which he finds uncertain or unique. He reflects on the phenomena before him, and on the prior understandings which have been implicit in his behavior. He carries out an experiment which serves to generate both a new understanding of the phenomena and a change in the situation.
>
> When someone reflects-in-action, he becomes a researcher in the practice context. He is not dependent on the categories of established theory and technique, but constructs a new theory of the unique case. His inquiry is not limited to a deliberation about means which depends on a prior agreement about ends. He does not keep means and ends separate, but defines them interactively as he frames a problematic situation. He does not separate thinking from doing, ratiocinating his way to a decision which he must later convert to action. Because his experimenting is a kind of action, implementation is built into his inquiry. Thus reflection-in-action can proceed, even in situations of uncertainty or unique-

ness, because it is not bound by the dichotomies of Technical Rationality (Schön 1983, 68–69).

Shortly I want to turn to two cases that illustrate many aspects of what Schön has described. Before doing so, however, let me emphasize two additional points about reflective practice.

First, while the process of reflective practice is similar enough across various professions to allow him to describe it, Schön recognizes that reflective practitioners differ in their approach to similar problems not only between professions but also within the same profession. What causes these differences? He suggests (Schön 1983, 274ff.) that they are caused by variations in at least four factors that various practitioners bring to their reflection-in-action:

> differences in the media, languages, and repertoires that practitioners use to describe reality and conduct their experiments (e.g., architects use sketch pads; engineers use models and experimental drawings; clergy or social workers use dialogue and interactive relationships);

> differences in the values (Schön's word is "appreciative systems") that professionals bring to the setting and reflective conversation and that they use to frame the situation initially, which set bounds on appropriate ends and means, and by which they judge results;

> differences in the overarching theories by which practitioners make sense of phenomena (theories do not supply specific solutions to problems but supply language by which to describe and interpret problems);

> differences in role frames within which they set their tasks.

While the first has primarily to do with differences among professions, the other three also apply to differences within professions and are particularly important to my interest in the visioning dimension of reflective leadership. Indeed, the clergy professional's values are central to shaping a vision of Christian existence and his or her understanding of the purpose of the church. Additionally, the knowledge and theories that one has learned—drawn from scripture and tradition, from the study of theology, from the social sciences and elsewhere—supply language by which one makes sense of the phenomena one encounters. Finally, how the clergyperson frames his or her primary task—for example, as evangelist, prophet, teacher, pastor, or administrator—also influences his or her vision for the church as well as the ways that he or she engages in reflection-in-action or discernment. I will return to these issues, resources for constructing practice, in the following chapter.

The other point that Schön makes has relevance to the relational dimension of authority. His observation of professionals who function reflectively led him to conclude that the authority of reflective practitioners differs from the traditional model of professional authority. The reflective professional has authority, but it is not the type that requires unquestioning trust in the professional's expertise or the kind of deference that such authority seems to demand. Rather, the professional and client (read "congregation" for client in the case of clergy) enter into a "reflective contract" (Schön 1983, 298f.). They join in a mutual effort to understand and find solutions to the issues confronting the client. The client agrees to confront the practitioner with what he or she does not understand, to make public the criteria for judging effectiveness, and to support, reward, and express appreciation for competent performance. Practitioners bring to the relationship their particular knowledge and reflective expertise, which they agree to use to the best of their ability for the good of the client. They treat the others not as dependent clients but as people who bring their own insights, gifts, and reflective capacities to the setting. They make themselves vulnerable to the client's questioning and critique, and they are willing to reflect publicly on the meanings of their counsel and advice. All of this means, as Schön (1983, 299) notes, that the reflective professional

> gives up the rewards of unquestioned authority, the freedom to practice without challenge to his competence, the comfort of relative invulnerability, the gratifications of deference. The new satisfactions open to him are largely those of discovery—about the meanings of his advice to clients, about his knowledge-in-practice, and about himself.

In short, the reflective practitioner has substituted the typically asymmetrical authority relationships, for which the professional model has been criticized, for a relatively symmetrical model where there is considerable mutuality and sharing in the resolution of the "messy" issues of practice.

Let me attempt now to bring this somewhat abstract discussion down to earth, so to speak, by using two concrete illustrations from ministry practice.

COLCHESTER ONCE MORE

Consider again the Colchester Church case introduced in the last chapter. It illustrates particularly well the interplay of vision and discernment and helps to make clear in a ministry situation many of the characteristics of reflection-in-action.

When Davida Crabtree accepted the call to the Colchester congregation, she was committed to a vision of the church that emphasized the ministry of the whole people of God. Under the model of technical rationality, her first step might have been to search out the best means for realizing that end. For example, she might have started by searching out a model for facilitating lay ministry, such as that of the Church of the Savior in Washington, D.C. Then she would have attempted to replicate it straightforwardly in the Colchester parish, much as, for example, some clergy take the latest theories and techniques of church growth and try to apply them. That was not what happened, and, had she tried it, she would probably have failed badly, as have a considerable number of congregations that have tried to import a Church of the Savior or other distinctive congregational model directly into their setting. Her vision of a church where ministry is shared and the actual situation existing in the Colchester congregation were considerably far apart, as is usually the case when a pastor comes into a new parish. The process was much slower, and it involved quite a bit of reflection-in-action, including the need to frame and reframe the problem several times.

Her first months in the parish were more in the nature of Schön's exploratory experiments: efforts to understand the lay of the land in the parish and community; efforts to assess possible starting points and roadblocks to implementing the vision; efforts, in short, to frame the problem that she and the parish faced if they were to work towards shared ministry in a way appropriate to Colchester. Is the realization of such a vision possible? Or is it wishful thinking?

She discovered, for example, that a previous controversy had led to a split in the congregation, with a number of young families leaving the church to form a more evangelical congregation. This, in turn, had led to considerable reluctance on the part of remaining members to talk about faith matters for fear of giving offense. There was also membership diversity between the older, long-term members who were mostly farmers and small-business persons, and newer members who worked in management and production jobs in a nearby city. These people reflected contrasting social and cultural backgrounds that did not make for easy communication. Further, she discovered that in Colchester, as in many other churches, there was a widely held assumption that the church had little to do with public life, including one's work life. Its concerns were mainly private. This early talkback from the congregation was important as she sought to lead.

Her first efforts to frame the issue led her and some of her lay leaders who shared her vision to conclude that a programmatic response was the best way to proceed. That included preaching on the ministry of the laity, the retreat "Discovering Our Gifts," and the conference on lay ministry described in the last chapter. Some of the ideas and materials used were drawn from her past experience as well as from others working at lay ministry issues. Although successful in beginning to raise the consciousness of a part of the congregation, she was aware that these means were not reaching a significant portion of the members. She met resistance at a number of points. This led to further reflection and a reframing of the issue, which included the recognition that retreats and conferences were geared more to the middle class and managerial styles. They were less part of the experiences of lower middle-class, blue-collar workers who constituted a significant portion of those relatively untouched by the programs. As a result, the pastor and her lay leadership group adopted new strategies of "listening teams," covenant groups, the pastor's "shadowing" members at their work settings, and a greater intentionality to relate faith and daily life in the Sunday services.

While these strategies bore fruit, she and the lay leaders began to be aware of a deeper problem, which led to yet another reframing of the issue: They recognized that the various programs for implementing the vision are add ons, that is, not really integral to the regular church organization. In sociological terms, they need to be institutionalized, given a more permanent home in the ongoing life of the church, or they risk being easily dropped. Additionally, they realized that the way the church operates places most of the emphasis on the use of one's gifts and resources to maintain the church's gathered life—a "come" structure rather than a "go out" structure. Thus, this new reframing of the issue has led her and the lay leaders to see the situation not simply as one that can be solved by developing new programs; it also involves a change in structures and processes that support the vision rather than work against it. They are now working to develop and implement a new management system for the parish to accomplish these ends. This, in itself, is an ongoing process involving continued reflection-in-action by both the pastor and the leaders of the congregation. It has also involved use of an outside consultant to assist them in assessing how far they have come toward realizing their vision and in thinking through the next steps.

This particular example of reflective leadership took place over a period of several years. The model of reflective leadership is, however, also applicable in much more time-limited situations, such as a pastoral counseling session, an issue that arises in the midst of a board or committee meeting, or even those tasks that one does as repetitively as the weekly discipline of sermon writing.[3] While the time frame in these situations may be much shorter than the one in Colchester, the basic exercise of authority, leading by reflection-in-action, is much the same. Also, unlike the Colchester example, things do not always work out to the satisfaction of those involved. Consider the following example, which is both short-term and not especially successful.

A FRUSTRATING ENCOUNTER WITH A PARISHIONER

This incident reflects a difficult pastor-parishioner relationship. It nevertheless gives insight into how the pastor engages in reflection-in-action in the course of an encounter with the parishioner. In the pastor's reconstruction of the incident, she has used a method for reflecting on instances of practice proposed by Argyris and Schön (1974, 41).[4]

The pastor, "Martha," is the senior minister of an old, prestigious United Church of Christ congregation in a large city. Though having suffered significant membership decline, as have other urban congregations, the church has a long history of activism in behalf of social justice issues, which it continues. It also has a significant endowment that helps to support its ministry and mission.

Not long before this particular conversation took place, the congregation had asked the Trust Committee, which oversees the investment of the church's endowment, for a report on the church's position regarding social responsibility in investment. They asked especially about South Africa and defense issues. The committee chairperson, "Alison," is an elderly woman who, along with another contemporary on the committee, has resisted dealing with the congregation's request and minimized the importance of divestment.

Alison and Martha have had an uneven relationship over the two and one half years that she has been pastor of the congregation. Alison campaigned against Martha's candidacy at the time of her call to the church, and the two have had other conflicts prior to the divestment issue.

Alison is in declining health. She lives alone and is increasingly unable to participate in the day-to-day life of the church. As an accommodation to Alison's limited mobility, the Trust Committee meets in her apartment instead of at the church, where all other church meetings are held. The apartment is small, dark, and overheated. There aren't enough chairs. All but one on the committee have confided to the pastor that they are uncomfortable in the setting and would rather not attend the long, frustrating, and often hostile meetings, which Alison dominates. Martha shares this attitude, but she is also ambivalent. She wishes that she could relate to Alison more positively and minister to her in such a way that the church could be a source of comfort to her rather than an aggravation.

On the day of the Trust Committee meeting, Martha discovers that she has a scheduling conflict that makes it impossible for her to attend the meeting. She calls Alison to inform her of her dilemma.

MARTHA: Hello, Alison. This is Martha. How are you today?

ALISON: So-so.

M: Are you still not feeling any better?

A: It is hard to tell. This is a long pull. But, I am a fighter, as you well know. I don't and won't give up!

M: At the Board meeting last week you said you were "about the same." It must be discouraging not to see any improvement.

A: It is discouraging, but I try to look on the bright side of things—that's my nature.

How are you? You've certainly been looking very well these days.

M: Well, that's good to hear! I'm feeling well, better actually. For some reason, I was depressed in September, but my energy seems to have returned and my spirit is more optimistic. I think for awhile I was preoccupied with the an-

Alison will not reveal any real information about her condition. In the past, she has alluded to its being a recurrence of earlier trouble, but that is all she will say. I resent having to cast about for details. Are we talking about something life threatening or something inconvenient? I want to express concern but sense she does not want to confide in me.

Maybe if I model some vulnerability and let her into my life somewhat, she'll let me into hers. I'll let her minister to me first.

niversary of Daddy's death more than I realized.

A: It takes a long time to get over that sort of loss. I know. I think you came back too fast and didn't give yourself enough time in the first place.

M: That may be true. I tend to be gentler with others than I am with myself. But, in a curious way, working was a real comfort to me, and in a sense, my work was my grief at that point. I had to live it with integrity, and still do. I hope I will be a better pastor for it.

I'm feeling defensive. Alison was one who complained that I took a week off! I feel as if I need to shore up my credibility and let her know that I know what I'm doing.

It's not as if I work in a bank or some place that doesn't value human process or feelings. And the church has been great. Our society moves so fast that sometimes we forget folk carry burdens and heartaches. But the church is different from that. We have a covenant to check in with one another and allow ourselves to be real and vulnerable and share the heaviness of our hearts.

Maybe I can do some education here. "Covenant" is a meaningful word for Alison, given her devotion to Congregationalism. I might be able to suggest in this way that, if she'd open up, maybe the church could help her with whatever is wrong.

(Silence)

M: Alison, if there is anything I or the church can do for you during this time, we want to do it. Do you need transportation? Help with marketing?

A: Thank you. It is a problem that I have to solve. It's not easy. I have things to be thankful for.

M: I respect your privacy, Alison. I just want you to know that I care about you and want to help, even it is just chatting over a cup of tea.

(Silence)

M: Alison, I need to talk with you about the Trust Committee meeting. I have a scheduling problem that I hope you can help me with. There is a community meeting about the drug traffic in the area near the church. I would like to attend, especially in light of the board's recommendation that I get involved in activities beyond the local church.

A: This is an important meeting of the Trust Committee!

M: I agree. The Trust Committee *is* important. That is why I'm calling. Could we go over your agenda so I can make an informed decision about where to be tonight?

A: As I hope you know, JR and PL are going to be with us, and it is very important that we meet with them. While they are here, we will talk about investment goals, and they also have some information about the most recent [name of a bank] fiasco. I'd like to get the custodian is-

I can't get in where I am not wanted. But neither will I entirely give up.

She is going to be mad! But, if I approach this asking for help, maybe she will feel included in the decision and valued for it. And maybe she will respond favorably to evidence that I am taking the board's evaluation of my ministry seriously.

The meetings are useless. She controls the agenda to the point of not having additional copies for members. Nothing of value happens. The investment counselors go crazy, and everyone is frustrated because Alison can't absorb the details or grasp the larger financial stewardship issues.

It embarrasses me that JR and PL, very high-powered partners in an investment advisory firm, are exposed to this "snake pit" of personality conflicts and internal church

sue cleared up. You know, Mary started all this and now she is not cooperating in resolving it.

M: I know that after researching the ins and outs of changing custodians, Mary reconsidered her original position and is not convinced that to change at this point is necessarily beneficial to the church. I think she is as frustrated as you are with all of this, Alison.

Tell me, the discussion of the goals—that will include consideration of the social responsibility and budget needs. Is there anything else?

A: No, that is the meat of it. But, I would like for us to talk about some positive aspects of investment for a change.

M: What do you mean?

A: I am sick and tired of all these accusations about South Africa! All this negativity! Let's concentrate on some of the good that we are doing.

M: It would be exciting for the committee to think about what it affirms in its investment policies and if there are places like community development projects or medical research projects, for example, where we could be intentional about our financial

problems such as the custodian issue. In fact, it is my suspicion that neither Mary nor Alison would be involved in the church were it not for the endowment and their involvement with it!

Alison carries the congregation's request that the Trust Committee report to it regarding social responsibility in our investments on the agenda of every meeting, but she spends so much time on things like setting the date for the next meeting, that we never get to it!

Alison and her one ally on on the committee have resisted consideration of divestment in South Africa, and their arguments and attitude have discouraged the other members. But maybe there is an opening here that can be used to help Alison see the issue in a different light.

involvement. You could offer some prophetic leadership in this area, Alison. It would be great to look at the good we could do with these resources, because the church is called to affirm life in all its activities, isn't it?

A: Yes, but it is one thing to be naive, and it is another to be rigorous about our financial responsibilities. We can't in good conscience take money out of IBM and put it in some small operation that will go bankrupt! You people don't understand all the issues here!

I can't win! Arguing the case has not worked in the past. Discussing the issues, point by point, is impossible. The only thing I can do may be to encourage any positive movement and hope to outlast her!

M; Alison, I only meant to encourage your leadership around the issue of positive investments. I think it represents a whole new way to think about the work of the Trust Committee.

As you know, I think there are other issues that are more important than the highest return or most secure investment. But, I am only one member of the committee, and ex officio at that. But, that's the special dimension of our congregational way— you add your insight and I add mine, and, the Holy Spirit willing, somewhere in that process, perhaps a bit more truth will shine for both of us. I am just happy to learn that you are open to consider-

I really don't believe that Alison's position on this issue is going to enlighten mine or that this is a positive example of free church polity. But neither am I interested in fighting with Alison about it. I decided some time ago to try to be her pastor, and not her prodder, on stuff like this. If I can bond with her on this commitment to group process, then I am ahead on my agenda, even if it is not the church's agenda.

ing some alternative investments. As I said earlier, I
think that is faithful, strong
leadership.

I am sorry that I won't be able
to attend the Trust Committee
meeting, but I am sure that
this evening's conversation
will continue next month.

A: You've decided not to come
to the meeting?

M: It sounds to me as if you
have the agenda well in hand.
I think I will attend the community drug meeting. Per-
haps I'll be able to contribute
and make a difference there.

When I heard myself saying
this, I realized how discouraged I feel in this relationship
and with Alison's leadership
in this important part of the
church's life. For me to think
that I might contribute more
to the crack crisis than I can in
my own parish is fairly damn-
ing, I think.

The format of this example provides us with a window into the reflective process (or at least a reconstruction of it). While it differs considerably from the
Colchester case in focus, time frame, and outcome, we
can nevertheless see similar elements of reflection-in-
action.

Martha brings several things to the encounter that
shape the way she frames the issue. There is her history
of past experiences with Alison, which fosters Martha's
ambivalence and her assumption that the call will be difficult. Martha also brings two assumptions about the
church and her role as pastor, which also foster ambivalence about how to proceed. On one hand, as she tells
Alison, "the church is called to affirm life in all its activities." This view expresses her vision of ministry and is
consistent with the identity of that particular congrega-

tion, with its long history of involvement in issues of justice and reconciliation. It also leads her to frame her own role in terms of involvement in community activities. Indeed, the congregation's board has encouraged that role. On the other hand, she believes that the church should be "a source of comfort and strength" to its members. In this perspective, Martha's role is that of pastor who loves Alison and ministers to her in spite of her obstreperousness. These two images of the church are not, in principle, contradictory. One has more to do with the church's public ministry, the other more with belonging and support. In this particular instance, however, they come into conflict and also create role conflict for Martha.

Alison too has framed the issue (though we are not privy to her reflection-in-action). Whatever else she believes about the church, she too wants it to function responsibly, though in terms of prudent and pragmatic fiscal responsibility, which is at odds with the call for socially responsible investment. While her behavior and need for control contradict her definition of fiscal responsibility, she nevertheless seems to frame the issue in these terms. She also frames the pastor's role in similar terms. The pastor ought to be giving pragmatic attention to the church's financial matters, though Alison views the pastor and others in the church who are calling for socially responsible investments as naive: "You people don't understand all the issues here!"

Although the purpose of the call is to inform Alison that she will not attend the meeting, Martha first frames the situation and her role in pastoral terms. While this may be a way of "softening" the anticipated conflict, it also reflects her concern to minister to Alison. In her pastoral frame, she conducts a frame experiment: She tries to model vulnerability, hoping that this will allow mutual ministry to occur. When it does not work out in the way that she had hoped, she tries another tack, using covenant language from the Congregational tradition to try to encourage mutuality. This, too, is a kind of move-taking experiment.

Failing once more to make headway from the pastoral frame, Martha shifts the conversation to the Trust Committee meeting. At this point, her understanding of the church's social justice responsibility and her role as community activist come into play and frame the issue for her. She reveals her scheduling conflict and reminds Alison of the board's request that she be active in community affairs. When Alison protests and recalls the importance of the Committee meeting, Martha's reflections reveal her frustration. She nevertheless tries another frame experiment—this time from the social justice frame. She affirms the importance of the Trust Committee's work and reminds Alison of the congregation's request for social accountability. She also encourages Alison to see the possibilities for prophetic leadership in her role as committee chairperson. Alison, however, will not buy into this perspective.

In continuing frustration, Martha recognizes that she is not going to win. Though she had hoped to resolve the situation in win-win terms, she realizes that, for Alison, it is a zero-sum game: One of them must lose. Unlike Jacob, who finally got the blessing from the angel, Martha cannot win Alison's blessing, either for her decision or for the social responsibility proposal. Thus, she once more reframes the encounter, returning to the pastoral frame. Again she draws on Congregational tradition in an effort to affirm Alison pastorally: "You add your insight and I'll add mine, and, the Holy Spirit willing, . . . perhaps a bit more truth will shine. . . . "

What can Martha (and we) learn from this encounter? Here is how she described her learnings:

> One can improve relationships and develop trust—
> get the blessing from the struggle—even with the
> most pernicious and obstreperous. (This is not necessarily true. Neither is it a healthy assumption. But

I operate out of it in this relationship. Alison "hooks" me. She threatens me. I want her approval and appreciation, and it aggravates me no end that she withholds it.)

One inherits a history when beginning a ministry, and that history is fraught with human frailties. Alison feels displaced and threatened by me. She has become marginalized in the organization. One way to bridge this emotional distance is to involve her as a partner in ministry instead of further isolating her.

Sometimes one has to make a decision about what is most important in a relationship. I have decided that the person is more valuable (for the time being) than some of the other issues and that her needs for control are deep and I must love her in spite of them. I am aware that by buying into this, I am colluding with very unhealthy patterns in the church and that I am compromising the institution, and I resent it. But, for a variety of reasons, I have decided to outlast her and make the best of it in the meantime.

Parish ministry can be the most frustrating, humiliating, and infuriating work in the world. What makes it rich—the complex mosaic of relationships—is also what often makes it impossibly slow.

Money is power. Information is power. Whoever controls these commodities controls a lot, even in the church!

These are candid and helpful post facto reflections-on-action. For the most part, they are not stated in biblical or specifically theological categories. Perhaps to have attempted to do so more explicitly would have helped Martha reflect more fully on her underlying vision of ministry and the tensions that existed in her efforts to frame her own role with Alison. Even without this, her reflections-on-action, along with other insights that came from colleagues when she presented the case in a class, have become part of her repertoire of theories and examples for future practice. While she was not successful in this instance in achieving hers or the congregation's ministry goals, her efforts to exercise leadership provide a helpful window into the reflective process. One does not move from theory to practice in a linear, technically rational fashion. One leads, or attempts to do so, by reflecting in the midst of action, bringing vision and discernment together with a kind of artistry that has a rigor and discipline of its own. Such a discipline can be learned—not, however, as a set of steps or formulae to be applied. That would be a reversion to technical rationality. Let me attempt to state more systematically what is involved if a pastor wishes to develop the capacity for reflective leadership or if a seminary wishes to teach students to become reflective leaders.

7

THE STRUCTURE
OF
REFLECTIVE LEADERSHIP

"For now we see in a mirror dimly . . . . Now
we know in part."
                                    —1 Corinthians 13:12

"Likewise the Spirit helps us in our weakness
. . . [and] intercedes for us with sighs too deep
for words."
                                    —Romans 8:26

Would all pastors have interpreted the situation in
Colchester or responded in the same way as Davida
Crabtree? Would their approach to Alison have been the
same as Martha's? The answer is almost certainly no.
That clergy (or laity) may differ considerably in the way
they interpret and act in situations seems so taken for
granted, so much a truism, that we may wonder if it
deserves mention. Before we agree too quickly, however,
I want to consider the implications of this taken-for-
granted assumption for ministry practice. Then, I examine some of the key resources available to us as we attempt to lead reflectively.

148

A CONSTRUCTIONIST VIEW OF PRACTICE

In contrasting practice based on technical rationality and that based on reflection-in-action, Donald Schön (1984, 18) points to constrasting underlying assumptions about reality.[1] Technical rationality is based on an *objectivist* view of reality and the practitioner's relation to it. Reflection-in-action, which is at the heart of reflective leadership, expresses a *constructionist* view. These two views of reality are also pertinent to the practice of ministry, especially if one recognizes them as forming poles of a continuum.

For a simple way of summarizing the spectrum from objectivist to constructionist, recall the three baseball umpires described in chapter 1. The first, clearly representing the objectivist position, calls them "as they are." The second is a moderate constructionist or perspectivalist: "I call them as I see them." But for the third, the radical constructionist, "they ain't nothing till I call them." At the risk of considerable oversimplification, let me describe the two extremes.

The objectivist assumes that there is a way to approach the practice of one's profession that is independent of the professional. It is objective, "out there," waiting to be known and applied: "I call them as they are." Professional practice involves learning the objective truth, based on the facts, and how this truth is to be applied in various instances of practice. If disagreements arise between practitioners, they can be resolved by reference to this body of knowledge or a better understanding of the facts. In this view, professional education— medical, legal, theological, or other—aims at providing aspiring practitioners with the most accurate, scientifically derived, objective knowledge currently available. The goal is to educate professionals who can apply their expertise in a straightforward, unambiguous way to achieve the ends of professional practice, whether those be health, justice, or salvation.

In contrast, constructionists believe that reality is always to some extent constructed by us and the communities to which we belong. The knower and the known are intimately and inescapably related. The extreme constructionist assumes that there is no objective reality that exists independently of the knower: "They ain't nothing 'til I call them." Reality and truth are always dependent on the knower, whether the knower is an individual or a group sharing a similar perspective.

In its more moderate expression, constructionists are still highly perspectival: "I call them as I see them." We always view situations from our particular vantage point, which shapes, colors, and frames what we see. We can learn to appreciate another's perspective or frame. We may even adopt the other's perspective and throw out our own because the other's seems to make more sense of things than our own, but our new understanding remains perspectival. Both forms of constructionism acknowledge the historicity of our knowledge described in chapter 1.

Professional knowledge and practice is, in the constructionist view, also perspectival, constructed by us as we bring our particular lenses to the situation. We are likely to hold different perspectives on the ends of practice and the means to those ends. We can make judgments about the rightness, adequacy, or effectiveness of ends or means based on fundamental assumptions that we make about reality, or on traditions to which we ascribe, or on the theories and discoveries of others. Our judgments, however, remain relative. They are constructions that we make from our particular vantage point as we participate in the knowing process and engage in reflection-in-action.

Our constructions are not simply subjectivistic and atomistic, as the above paragraphs might imply. Were that the case, we would live in anarchy. This is so for two reasons. First, we share a culture with others in our society or region. We also share a culture with others in our religious tradition, including our congregation. This shared culture(s) provides us with language and other symbols, shapes our world view and perceptions, and makes it possible for us to communicate. In most cases, we see and know what our particular culture prepares us to see and know.

Second, another kind of mutuality also saves reflective leadership from subjectivism and atomism, the mutuality of knower and known. Truth is neither "out there," independent of the knower, nor is it "in here," totally subjective. Rather, it is between the knower and known, whether the known be another self or the material world. Writing on the relation of spirituality and education, Parker Palmer (1990, 55f.) observes that

> Truth is between us, in relationship, to be found in the dialogue of knowers and knowns who are understood as independent but accountable selves. This dialogue saves personal truth from subjectivism, for genuine dialogue is possible as I acknowledge an integrity in the other that cannot be reduced to my perceptions and needs.

This is another reminder that the authority that the reflective leader exercises is relatively symmetrical. It is based on mutuality, where truth is found in the reflective conversation with the situation, including those others who are part of it.

How does all this apply to leadership in the church? Does it matter whether we exercise authority as objectivists or constructionists? Obviously it does, and this is an issue that we must not pass over lightly. While most may agree that different pastors will approach particular situations differently, and that this is true of most cases of pastoral practice, objectivists and constructionists will nevertheless differ in how they account for this variability. Let me risk caricature to make the point.

For the objectivist, there really is a correct way to

respond in any given pastoral situation, whether in defining meaning, building community, or empowering the church's public ministry. A rational approach to practice exists where ends and means are relatively unambiguous. If there are significant differences in the actual responses of different pastors or laity, it is because they possess an inadequate knowledge of the truth, or, worse, because they are spiritually blind.

For some objectivists, truth is found in a literal interpretation of the scriptures. This is the way of the biblical inerrantist. He or she believes that the scriptures are the literal words of God that the Holy Spirit will lead one to discover and apply in every situation that arises.[2] For others, truth is found in strict adherence to the church's tradition, especially in those matters of faith and practice on which a supreme authority such as the pope has spoken infallibly or that have the weight of a church council behind them. One of the important struggles taking place in contemporary Catholicism is over an increasingly objectivist stance to which Pope John Paul II is calling Catholics, including Catholic theologians, to adhere.

While not biblical literalists or Catholic traditionalists, many church leaders have exhibited yet another objectivist approach. I referred in chapter 5 to H. Paul Douglass' notion of scientific churchmanship, whereby one discovers and applies the "laws" of how churches function. While they may not use Douglass' phrase to describe themselves, many clergy seem to hold to a similar point of view. An example is those pastors who take the discoveries and theories of church consultants and researchers as gospel truth with universal applicability. I am regularly dismayed at how some pastors and church leaders cite the works of a consultant such as Lyle Schaller, for example—whose insights I greatly respect—with a reverence approaching that of a fundamentalist for the Bible.

The constructionist—and it should be obvious that I place the reflective leader in this type—will approach situations of pastoral practice with much less certainty that there is one best way to respond. This need not imply a relativist assumption that all responses are equally valid. Rather, one will function much as the reflective leaders described in the previous chapter. One will be guided by his or her basic convictions about God and God's purposes, such as the criteria from Jesus' ministry described in chapter 4. These convictions are informed by scripture and by church traditions, the practices of Christians in other times and places. One will also draw on the theories and insights of the social sciences and of students of present-day church practice. One will likewise draw on his or her own experience in other situations. And one will be guided by the truth that comes from others in the situation. For the constructionist, however, these resources do not move from theory to practice but are part of a reflective conversation with each ministry situation. It is not a matter of finding the *one* correct response, but rather of finding—in the midst of practice—a response that is faithful to one's understanding of the gospel and to the unique character and dynamics of the particular situation. This is how God's Spirit guides us in the construction of ministry practice in those situations where we "see in a mirror dimly."

What does this imply for authority? The one who takes the objectivist point of view—whether from scripture, tradition, or scientific churchmanship—has a more secure basis for her or his authority as a leader, especially when others in the situation share similar convictions about scripture, tradition, or "laws" of church practice. Then one can simply quote chapter and verse of scripture, cite the tradition, or cite a rule of church practice, and apply these objective truths to the situation.

For the reasons discussed in chapter 1, such an objectivist approach is simply not viable for many of us today. Authoritative leadership is no less needed, but it will be the kind of reflective leadership that I am attempting to describe. *The authority of the reflective leader*

*resides in her or his ability to assist partners in ministry to
form a vision of Christian existence and construct responses
that are both faithful to that vision and appropriate within
the complex, messy situations of practice.* Such situations
rarely lend themselves to simple, clear-cut answers!

Let us consider, therefore, some of the key resources
on which we draw as we construct our practice. I introduce the discussion by drawing on another case of ministry practice.

ESTABLISHING MINISTRY PRIORITIES

"John" serves a Lutheran church located in an urban neighborhood in a medium-sized city. The city is
characterized by sharp disparities between its affluent
suburbs and its impoverished central city. The congregation's approximately two hundred and fifty members are
mostly white middle- and lower middle-class. Many are
middle-aged or older, and some commute to the church
from the suburbs. At the time of the initial discussion
reported below, approximately 17 percent of the members were African-American, many of whom lived in the
neighborhood around the church.

John, formerly a campus minister, accepted the call
to the congregation because he was excited about the
possibility for urban ministry that he saw for himself and
for this particular congregation. His training, experience,
and theological commitments had led him to a dynamic
vision of the church's ministry in an urban setting and
what that implied for his role as pastor. As he described
it, "I looked forward to engaging myself and the congregation with some of the rude issues of the city, reaching
out to the downtrodden and oppressed, being a beacon
of hope . . . ."

In campus ministry, he had experienced a congregation that combined a transient student population and a
more stable membership, many of whom were not uni-

versity-related but were attracted to a university church. As he came to his new congregation, he hoped that something analogous to this model might also develop. He hoped that there would be a mix of neighborhood people, many of whom were low income and, like the students, somewhat transient, and a more stable core of suburban residents who would "drive by six or seven churches to come to the urban setting where something exciting was going on."

In the five years since coming to the church, he has realized a part of this vision. He has been a visible and highly effective clergy leader within the city, working with various organizations concerned with the quality of urban life. His congregational members have affirmed and supported him in this role. They are happy with his leadership, especially with his preaching and liturgical leadership, and they are proud of the work he does as a representative of the church in the city. Furthermore, they have endorsed his proposal to call an African-American associate pastor.

At an informal breakfast meeting where John and several clergy colleagues gather regularly for sharing and support, John laid out a number of issues that trouble him. He is troubled that much of the ministry involvement in the city is primarily his own, not that of many of his members. They support him in his efforts but do not often join him in the ministry except vicariously. He is also perplexed by a growing awareness that the congregation's internal life needs much more attention than he has given it or can give it if he is to maintain his ministry in various aspects of urban life. He ticked off a number of what he called "infrastructure" issues. The building requires substantial fixing up, from peeling paint to broken toilets. The music program and the church school are "in a state of crisis." Boards and committees need to plan and set priorities, but members find such activities alien to their style. New leaders need to be developed, but

there is little enthusiasm for training workshops or retreats—for some of the same reasons that Colchester
members also lacked enthusiasm.

He is especially concerned about the church's relative lack of success in attracting significant numbers of
new members. Some new members have come from
the neighborhood—primarily low-income African-
Americans—but many are transient. "It's like a rotating
door," he says. Nor has there been much influx of new
members driving in from the suburbs. Of the new members that have come, many have little background in the
Lutheran tradition, and some have had no church background at all. All of these issues have left him feeling "a
little bit like the Dutch boy, putting the finger in the
dike." Giving needed attention to these issues competes
with his commitment to engagement in urban issues.

John's clergy colleagues affirmed both his vision of
the church and his own effectiveness in urban ministry.
At the same time, they responded to his concern over
infrastructure issues. In particular, they focused on the
issue of membership recruitment.

The discussion became quite lively when "Andy," a
strong advocate of church growth, suggested that a solu-
tion to John's infrastructure and membership problems
would be the adoption of a church growth agenda, using
the strategies of the church growth movement. Andy
noted that, when he came to his present congregation, he
understood his call to be that of building up the congregation's membership. In doing so he had to learn and use
the theories and techniques of church growth. They
would help John as well. "These are techniques that really work and that can bring in new members," Andy
asserted. "I have used them effectively, and I will be glad
to share them with you." In particular, Andy emphasized
the need to increase the number of middle-class members, those who have experience in dealing with some of
the infrastructure issues that John had noted. While this
need not preclude, in Andy's opinion, the congregation's

ministry to those experiencing various forms of oppression, John needs the organizational experience and skills of more middle-class members to share this ministry with him. "There are ways of accomplishing this," Andy continued. "If you do them, I believe you are going to grow. If you don't do them, I don't think you will grow. And it is not necessarily improving the quality of your ministry. In that, you've already got it over any of us. But these other things are really essential. . . . They are simple things that can be done and that anybody can do."

As they discussed the issue, it became quite clear that the costs of incorporating Andy's vision and strategies involved a greater price than John was willing to pay. In particular, he resisted focusing primary attention on attracting middle-class folk. He objected both on scriptural grounds and on the basis of his understanding of the church. At one point, he described his feelings this way: "We have right now a gem of a place so far as there being neither Jew nor Greek, male nor female . . . . It is an inspiration to me to see how this diversity is real. I think it is very precious, and I would be reluctant to charge out in some direction that would change the character of that, where like would attract like."

The discussion, of which I have only reported a short part, continued without any final resolution. John did agree, however, that he would consider making use of some of the church growth techniques and other strategies that would not violate his vision of an inclusive church, or of a vital urban ministry, or his sense of the centrality for Lutherans of Word and Table. He also recognized the necessity of devoting more energy to the other infrastructure issues that he identified.

In a review of his situation some months later, John confirmed that he has addressed infrastructure issues with seriousness and with several positive results. He has tried to do so without compromising his commitment to a vital urban ministry, congregational inclusiveness, or the centrality of Word and Sacrament. Attending to building

maintenance, for example, has taught him the importance for an urban congregation of a well-kept and at-
tractive building as a symbol, in Paul Tillich's sense of
the word. The building, he believes, points beyond itself
and participates in the reality of the kingdom to which
the church bears witness. A successful search for an African-American associate has also borne fruit in urban witness and in attracting a number of leaders from the
surrounding community to the church, who, in turn, are
sharing urban ministry with John and his associate.
While the nonwhite membership has increased to approximately 30 percent, the congregation's success in attracting suburbanites has been limited, and it continues
to struggle with some of the other infrastructure issues
that he had earlier identified.

Elements of Reflective Leadership

What can we learn from this vignette and from
other instances of ministry about the elements out of
which we construct our practice in reflective conversation
with the situation? The case illustrates two primary types
of resources. For want of better labels, I refer to them as
"background" and "foreground" resources. Those that I
label background are those that are somewhat more enduring parts of ourselves and the settings' makeup. They
are also often more tacit than explicit. In contrast, foreground elements are more situation-specific. Likewise,
they are more explicitly brought into play.[3]

In John's case, *background elements* include both his
and the congregation's past experiences. John brought
not only his own particular gifts for ministry, which are
considerable, but also a fairly well-formed and explicit
theology of ministry. He also brought with him past experiences—the campus ministry model, for example—
that had shaped his vision of a vital urban congregation.
Upon assuming his new role he did not, however, encounter the congregation as a blank slate on which he

could write whatever ministry scenario he wished. The church had a particular identity of its own, forged out of its past experiences, shaped by previous lay and clergy leaders, and reflecting its current members and context. Some of the infrastructure issues that John identified reflect the congregation's character as a small, middle- to lower middle-class, somewhat older congregation—for example, the resistance to planning and goal setting or to more formal efforts at leadership development. Both he and the congregation shared a Lutheran identity that affected their relationship and understanding of ministry, but many of the new members lacked this background and had to be socialized into it. The congregation also existed in a particular context, an inner-urban neighborhood in a medium-sized city characterized by considerable disparities between the city and its suburbs. This too had helped to shape its identity.

Foreground elements also come into play in the discussion among John and his colleagues. The colleagues, especially Andy, offered resources from their own experience and from various theories and techniques of church growth as ways of dealing with some of the infrastructure issues. In reflecting on their appropriateness, John drew on biblical and theological resources and insights from his Lutheran tradition. He and his colleagues also discussed specific aspects of the church's social context that affected the congregation's current membership and potential for new member growth. In short, both background and foreground resources became part of their reflective conversation about the situation.

BACKGROUND FACTORS

In his book *After Virtue*, Alasdair MacIntyre (1981, 194) illumines the importance of background factors for understanding a person or group's actions. He writes: "We identify a particular action only by invoking two kinds of context, implicitly if not explicitly. We place the agent's intentions . . . in causal and temporal order with reference to their role in his or her history; and we also place them with reference to their role in the history of the setting or settings to which they belong." Our intentions and actions are not atomistic units of behavior, nor are they simply the product of resources on which we draw explicitly in given instances. Rather, we must understand them in terms of the complex narratives of which they are a part: our personal narrative or story and the narrative or story of the setting in which we are functioning.

Consider this in dramaturgical terms. The pastor is an actor who brings his or her own characteristic way of playing the pastoral role into an ongoing congregational drama. The congregation's drama began before this particular pastor came to play the pastoral role, and it will probably continue with other pastoral actors after she or he has departed the scene. When the pastor enters a congregation, the script is not determined for either of them, pastor or congregation. Nevertheless, what has gone before in the experience of the pastor and the congregation and how each envisions the future of the drama set boundaries on and guide how together they construct the twists and turns of their now-intertwined plots.*

The Pastor's Story

Clergy who assume leadership of a congregation or function in any type of ministry setting do not come to these settings as ahistorical individuals or disembodied selves. The same is true for the laity in the setting. Each brings a history.

In part, that history includes an explicit (as in John's

---

*If I wanted to make this more complex than it already is, I should also acknowledge that each congregational member has an identity separate from that of the congregation or pastor, which also adds to the dynamics of the situation. For now, however, let us simply focus on the two identities, pastor and congregation.

case) or more implicit theological perspective, one's vision of Christian faith and life. I do not mean theology as an academic discipline, although various academic theologies may indeed help to shape one's basic theological perspective and aid one's reflection in particular moments of practice. I mean, rather, one's fundamental way of construing life from a faith perspective. Edward Farley (1983, 35f.) refers to this as *habitus*: theology as a kind of "a habit, an enduring orientation and dexterity of the soul." It is an existential, personal knowledge of God that gives shape to the way that one views the life of faith, one's own life, and the purpose of the church and its ministry. As such, *habitus* is not simply a matter of a clergyperson's expertise. It is a fundamental part of her or his being. It is also related to the other penultimate basis of clergy authority, representing the sacred, to which I return in the next chapter.

Theology, in this broad sense of *habitus*, plays an important role in the conversation with the situation in which the reflective leader engages. It shapes the leader's view of the ends of practice and contributes to the way she or he frames particular issues and her or his role in the situation. It also sets limits on what are appropriate or inappropriate ways of responding. We saw how theology as *habitus* entered into John's reflection about his ministry priorities; how it guided Davida Crabtree as she framed and reframed her practice in Colchester; and how it influenced Martha's struggles to define her role in relation to Alison. Their *habitus* did not determine what they did, in any definitive sense. It was not a theory that they applied. Yet it entered significantly into their reflective conversation with their situations. My effort in chapter 3 to spell out several assumptions about the church grows from my own vision of ministry and informs the way that I think about church practice.

Without such a basic vision of Christian faith and life, even when one does not articulate it fully, the result is an atheological approach to ministry. Other values—

for example, success, growth for growth's sake, efficiency, homogeneity—take precedence. Several of the vignettes in chapter 1 reflect this problem: the pastor who prides herself on a well-run church but whose lay members complain about a lack of vision and spiritual depth and another who finds herself running from meeting to meeting and who wonders, "What is it all for?"

Closely related to one's *habitus*—most likely reflecting it—is one's characteristic way of framing one's role as an ordained minister. While specific role frames will vary from circumstance to circumstance, most clergy have a primary frame through which they view themselves and exercise their ministry—John's image of himself as an urban pastor, for example. Samuel Blizzard (1985) referred to these role frames as "integrative roles." Integrative roles are goal-oriented images that one uses to describe what he or she is primarily trying to accomplish in professional relationships with parishioners, church associations, community groups, and the general public. For example, some frame their role as clergy primarily in terms of being a *spiritual guide* for the congregation, both by precept and the example of their own personal spiritual pilgrimage. Others may frame their role primarily as *servants of the Word*, focusing their ministry around preaching and teaching. Yet others see themselves principally in *priestly* terms, living in the midst of others as sacramental persons, mediating between God and humankind. Another primary integrative image is that of *pastor* or *shepherd*, or the more contemporary image of *pastoral counselor*. Or one may view his or her role in managerial terms as *parish developer*, administering and managing an effective, vital church organization. Another may understand his or her primary task as an *evangelist* or *witness*, while yet another may use *social action* and liberation images as primary.

While Blizzard found that each pastor typically has more than one integrative role that he or she calls on as circumstances demand, one is typically dominant. It influences how he or she sees most instances of practice. If one is not aware of other ways of framing the situation than one's usual way, or if one does not explore these alternative frames—even if they prove to be dead ends—one may miss important opportunities for leading in difficult, messy situations of practice. For example, John's colleagues helped him to see that framing his role in parish development terms would not necessarily subvert his primary role frame as urban pastor. Rather, it might help him to involve the congregation itself more effectively in urban ministry as its infrastructure is strengthened.

Our personal narratives also include a variety of nontheological elements, which likewise are important for our construction of practice: family influences, influences from the regional and ethnic culture in which we were raised, the impact of our social class or our gender, the effects of education, the impact of persons (including other pastors) who have been important role models, the impact of past experiences in other churches and ministry settings. As the sociology of knowledge makes clear, these elements play an important role in shaping our basic theological perspectives and the ways we construct interpretations of situations, frame our own role in them, and respond.

For example, the African-American experience of victimization, oppression, and injustice gives African-Americans a hermeneutic of suspicion that profoundly and justifiably shapes their construction of reality and interpretations. Similarly, both the feminist movement in general and recent studies of gender differences in particular have helped us to appreciate the important role that gender plays in shaping the way men and women construct situations, often in strikingly different ways.[4] Likewise, we are increasingly aware of the impact of generational differences on both behavior and interpretations of reality—for example, members of the baby boom generation had considerably different experiences during their formative years than those who grew up during the

Great Depression. Such historical experiences lead to distinctly different frameworks through which particular generations construct reality.[5]

We do not leave these elements of our personal story behind when we assume the clergy role or don our clerical garb, nor do laity leave their stories behind as they participate in congregational life. Whether we wear a Roman collar or a Geneva gown, these are not costumes behind which we can hide our personal identity. These may be important symbolic reminders that our authority derives ultimately from One who is other than our individual selves, but they do not permit us to escape being *"what one is never not,"* to use Erik Erikson's (1969, 266) description of one's identity.

The point is that we should not ignore these background resources as unimportant, but we should recognize their continuing power for good and for ill in affecting our ministry practice and our authority as clergy. Most of the time, they remain tacit rather than explicit in our practice. But as we become more explicitly aware of them and their influence, we are able to maximize their strengths and the insights they bring while minimizing their limitations, including the blind spots they encourage. The Socratic maxim "Know thyself" is basic to reflective leadership.

The Setting's Narrative

MacIntyre calls attention to a second background element: the narrative of the setting in which one acts. As John's case helps us to see, congregations themselves have narratives, each with their distinctive settings and cast of characters and each with a characteristic way of viewing the world and acting in it. It is through its particular and distinctive narrative expression that a congregation embodies itself as the body of Christ in its own particular time and place. As James Hopewell (1987, 16) expressed it, "Congregations everywhere are thick gatherings of complicated actions, each parish distinctive in its expression, each possessing its own genius yet incarnating in that peculiarity the worldly message and mission of Christ." Reflective leaders learn to lead from *within* the congregation's culture, not in disregard of it.

Congregational narratives often include the rich flavor of a particular ethnic history. They are shaped by important events in a congregation's life, saints and sinners in the congregation's past and present, and distinctive experiences that have influenced members' characteristic ways of responding to each other and to challenges and opportunities that confront them. Other congregational characteristics—membership size, the age of members, their resources, and elements of the congregation's context—also shape congregational narratives.

These events, experiences, characters, and characteristics mean that congregations, like people, differ in important ways, even when they share a common Christian and denominational heritage. Some have the self-image and style of high status churches—"old first" churches; others have a less exalted self-image—"little brown churches in the vale." Some congregations proclaim their denominational labels proudly—Calvin Presbyterian Church, Wesley Memorial United Methodist—others wear them lightly. Some proclaim their theological identity in their names—Solid Rock Independent Baptist Church, Grace Lutheran Church, Fire Baptized Pentecostal Holiness Church; others define themselves geographically—West Market Street United Methodist. Some congregations may be staid and formal in their worship style, others informal. Some regard themselves as an extended family; others seem little more than associations of individuals who have few ties beyond their congregational membership. Some congregations handle conflict by dealing with it openly; others do so by avoidance and denial, by keeping it under wraps. Some have a history of aggressive evangelism; others tend to say, "We're here. If you want to become a part of us, you must take the initiative." Some believe that congregational mem-

bers should experience a definite, "born again" conversion experience; others stress education and gradual
growth into faith.

In some congregations, it is expected that the pastor
will address the stewardship of money and church fi-
nances as spiritual issues; in others, it is a taboo for such
matters to be addressed in the context of worship. Some
congregations believe that it is appropriate for the congregation, qua congregation, to take an active role in
addressing social issues; others leave such action to individual members and prefer that the congregation, at best,
should help individuals to make informed decisions
about action. Some congregations view themselves as
sanctuaries, calling people to come apart from the world
for refreshment and renewal; others view themselves in
activist terms, some in aggressive evangelism, others in
efforts to promote social justice.[6] These are but a few of
the many ways in which congregations vary in self-
definition and in expressing their character. This cata-
logue of differences reminds us, however, that every
congregation has its own narrative and that its narrative
shapes how the congregation constructs reality, how
members frame situations, and how they respond to
change—sometimes, as with Alison, in sharp contrast to
the pastor.

Leaders often discover the deep structures of this
narrative when they attempt a change. When Davida
Crabtree began her initial efforts to foster lay ministry,
she found that members were reluctant to talk about
their faith, much less attempt connections between Sunday worship and Monday life. She discovered that some
of this reluctance was the result of a split in the congregation twenty years earlier in which a number of members left to form Bible Baptist Church. As noted, John's
congregation resists a planning and goal setting style,
though they do plan in their own way, and they are not
comfortable with retreats and workshops for leadership
training. These are foreign to their culture.

Not only efforts at change but conflicts and crises also reveal elements of a congregation's distinctive character. A conflict over the kind of hymns to be sung in the morning worship, debate about whether sacred dance should be permitted in worship, a moral failure on the part of the pastor, a controversy that arises when a prominent member wants to serve alcohol at her daughter's wedding reception in the church hall, the suicide of a prominent member—these are occasions in which a congregation's particular identity becomes apparent, often transparent. The deacons of one United Church of Christ congregation, with strong roots in the Congregational tradition, spent three years in fairly regular and often heated discussion over whether to accept the gift of a cross for use in the congregation's "meeting room," as traditional Congregationalists call their central place for worship. Did placing the cross there somehow violate the culture of Congregationalism, with its Puritan roots?

As James Hopewell (1987, 9ff.) reminds us, most of us have been trained to be embarrassed by these narrative structures we find in congregations, embarrassed by their all-too-apparent humanity. We have been trained to believe that some ideal congregation exists—perhaps to be found in the New Testament—that present-day congregations should be able to emulate. Against this ideal we hold up the human character of existing congregations and condemn them for their failure. Hopewell calls us, however, to recognize the ambiguity of human association present in all congregations, including those we find in the New Testament. He calls us, too, to accept the congregation's designation as the body of Christ: "The thick gathering of the congregation is much more than a hypocritical assembly; it is for Christians the immediate outworking of human community redeemed by Christ" (p. 11).

Clergy and others in the congregation who wish to lead reflectively have, therefore, a double task: They must be self-reflective about their own personal story (how it shapes their interpretations and responses in situations of practice); and they must also understand the narrative of the setting in which they minister (the congregation's characteristic way of framing situations).[7] These two elements, often in the background rather than foreground, are like the hidden mass of an iceberg. They can wreck us if we are not aware of them. If we take them into account, they can provide a solid base on which to build. In the dramaturgical metaphor, they profoundly influence the ongoing plot of the congregational drama for good or ill.

FOREGROUND FACTORS

Factors that are more in the foreground also come into play as we construct our ministry practice. These are resources about which we are often more explicitly aware. There are four to consider in particular: scripture and tradition, theories and exemplars from experience (one's own and those of others), elements of the setting or context, and talkback from the situation.

The Christian Story: Scripture and Tradition

Scripture and tradition may be treated together. They constitute the normative center of Christian story, of which each congregation is a particular local expression. I have already indicated that neither scripture nor tradition can be turned to for *objective truth*, untouched by the historicity that affects all of our knowledge. This means that neither constitutes a set of blueprints or templates that we can lay over contemporary issues of practice to tell us how to respond. Yet to acknowledge this does not reduce their role as a prime resource for constructing faithful ministry practice and congregational decision making. Both reflect the struggles of God's people to respond in faithfulness to the gospel under a broad range of circumstances.

From the beginning, and for good reason, the church has given primacy to scripture, first to the history and testimony of the Hebrew people and later, as the Christian canon was established, to that of the Christian communities of the first one hundred years following the birth of Jesus. From its confessional starting point the church has accorded these documents, both Old and New Testaments, an authority for belief and practice that exceeds those that follow. They recount the stories and teachings, especially those of Jesus, in whom we believe God and God's purposes for all of creation stand most clearly revealed. Thus the scriptures are the starting point, the lodestone that draws us to itself, as we seek to find patterns for assessing and constructing our ministry practice and the life and speech of the church today.

At the same time, however, God's Spirit has led communities of Christians to new constructions of practice and belief in the centuries following the apostolic era. These traditions, which record the subsequent struggles of Christians to be faithful as they faced new and different challenges, are also a significant resource for practice. I deliberately use the plural "traditions" to emphasize the multiple and often conflicting strands of teachings and actions that constitute the rich heritage on which we draw.[8]

In their discussion of the role of scripture and tradition in pastoral decision making, James and Evelyn Whitehead (1981, 14) note how recent theology, especially in the Roman Catholic Church, has moved from an older, static, ahistorical approach to scripture and tradition as a "deposit of faith," given once for all, to a perspective that focuses on the *process of traditioning* in both scripture and the subsequent history of the church. This newer emphasis is historical and dynamic and considers the formative presence of the Holy Spirit in leading God's people in their struggle for faithfulness under changing circumstances. As the hymn puts it, "new occasions teach new duties." The historical-critical approach to the scriptures (and also to the tradition) has helped us to take this more dynamic approach. More recently, the use of sociological and anthropological insights to study scripture and the church's subsequent history has enabled us even more to understand the dynamics of the traditioning process and the ways Christians have struggled with issues of faith and faithfulness.[9]

Thus both scripture and the subsequent thought and practice of the church are core resources for constructing practice. We have been much more likely to recognize this, especially the centrality of scripture, in our preaching and teaching roles. We have not done so well in other instances of practice. Yet they are equally important resources in all aspects of practice as they provide us with patterns or models for assessing the "Christian aptness" of contemporary practice, to use David Kelsey's helpful phrase (1975, 192). They give us examples of how God's people have addressed issues—sometimes in ways that we now judge to have been wrong or unfaithful—that are similar to those we continue to face. They also give us language by which we can frame issues of practice and assess various options for response. And they provide boundaries or parameters within which we may construct our own solutions to contemporary issues of ministry. But they do not let us off the hook of responsibility for our own construction of practice.[10]

Let me use an illustration from the experience of a pastor of a Church of God (Cleveland, Tennessee) congregation (Brooms, 1988). His predominantly African-American congregation had several important characteristics that were part of its identity: a strong, fundamentalist respect for the Bible and an inward focus on spiritual life and personal holiness with a corresponding resistance to social ministry. The congregation was located in an inner-urban neighborhood rife with drug dealing and poverty.

Participating in a doctor of ministry program, the pastor encountered in a new way the tradition of his denomination and of the broader Pentecostal-Holiness heritage. In particular, his imagination was captured by what David Moberg (1972) and others have called "the

Great Reversal"—that is, the shift, early in this century, of evangelical Christians from efforts to ameliorate the social evils of society to an almost exclusive focus on individual salvation. The more he read of his Pentecostal-Holiness heritage and the more he immersed himself in studying the biblical accounts of Jesus' ministry, the more he realized the inadequacy—the Christian *inapt*-ness—of his and his congregation's inward-looking focus. They were framing their ministry too narrowly and in ways that were unfaithful to both the scripture and the denomination's tradition. Consequently, in his preaching and teaching, he began to lead his congregation in a process of reflection and reframing which he referred to as "faithfulness to the whole Christ." Together they studied the scriptures, engaged their Pentecostal-Holiness tradition, brought in consultants from social agencies working in the community, and began to ask what following the "whole Christ" implied concretely for their ministry in the community. One small but important step was the start of a food pantry at the church; another was support for antidrug efforts in the community. Slowly but surely they began to reframe and reform their church practice by attention to the scriptures and the tradition in which they stood.

I will return below to the importance of knowledge of the context as a resource for practice. For now, I want to emphasize especially how important it was for this pastor and his congregation to assess their story in light of the gospel story and their denomination's heritage. These resources provided new models for them that, for all of their newness, were not alien to his or the congregation's identity. They were scripturally based and came out of their particular tradition. Thus new vistas opened for them that had not seemed possible before.

As this example makes clear, scripture and the traditions of the church provide points of leverage for change that may be hidden rather than manifest in a particular congregation's identity or story. While a particular congregation stands in the broader Christian story with its various subplots, it often ignores much of this broader story. Its focus is selective. As the pastor brought the neglected or hidden elements to his own and the congregation's consciousness, these neglected parts of the story connected with their story and judged the adequacy of their current practice. More important, they opened new possibilities of faithfulness that built on rather than denied their identity.

Medieval theologians referred to such hidden elements as a "shadow tradition." They meant by this those things that had been dropped, rejected, or neglected in the tradition, but nevertheless remain in the shadows. As such, these elements are available to living communities as important points of leverage for change. Today, Christian feminists are making especially important contributions to the life of the church as they reclaim parts of the shadow tradition reflecting women's experience. These aspects of the tradition have been hidden and neglected by the patriarchy that has pervaded the scriptures and subsequent Christian traditions. In this way, their personal narratives as women link with the broader Christian story. The hidden traditions come out of the shadows and provide leverage for critiquing and enriching both the traditions and present practice.

Theories, Models, and Exemplars

When faced with an issue of ministry practice, one of the first resources on which many of us draw—often disregarding our theological vision, the Bible and church traditions—are insights, theories, models, and exemplars from our own and others' experience. Especially included are theories, models, and techniques drawn from the subdisciplines of practical theology and from sociology, psychology, or organizational development. We draw too on models and examples of practice that others have found to be workable and on solutions that come from our own previous experiences with similar challenges. In particular, as I noted above, many clergy apply the techniques and theories of church consultants. Their remedies for curing ailing congregations and making them effective have become for church leaders what one of my colleagues calls a new type of wisdom literature. It is cited much more often than the wisdom literature of the scripture!

My frustration over the uncritical use of these resources should by now be evident. It reflects the worst of American pragmatism and technically rational assumptions about ministry. Andy's conviction that if John would just follow a few simple principles of church growth he could solve a major infrastructure problem illustrates a widespread tendency of clergy. But an opposite error would have been for John to ignore Andy's insights. Rather, John put them in conversation with other elements of the situation, including his understanding of the Christian story. Out of that conversation, he was able to construct a response that made critical use of Andy's and others' perspectives.

The point is that our reflective conversations are not monologues. They are, at the least, dialogues where theories, techniques, and exemplars are brought into conversation with the Christian story and our visions of Christian existence. They constitute an important resource for ministry practice. It is *a part*—not the whole—of the resources available to us. Drawing on these insights gives us models, tools for analysis, assistance in framing particular instances of practice, help in seeing connections (differences and similarities) between this situation and another, and options for the various kinds of experiments in which we engage as we construct responses that are faithful to the Christian story. Without them we would be much the poorer.

The Setting

At a workshop for field work supervisors and the seminary students who would be working with them, we

examined a case study that involved deciding what options for ministry existed in a particular situation. As part
of the discussion, I asked a number of questions about
the setting. I sensed a growing frustration among several
of the participants. Finally a student spoke up. "Let's cut
out all this sociological crap," she said. "What we need to
do is 'let the church be the church.' Let's give them
Christ, not statistics!" A pastor joined her protest and
reminded the group that the success of Kentucky Fried
Chicken consisted in selling the best possible chicken,
not in doing sociological analysis of their setting. I think I
understand something of their frustration. As with theories and techniques applied uncritically, so also can there
be a paralysis of analysis. Nonetheless, I strongly dis-
agree with the student and the pastor. I reminded the
pastor that his analogy was an especially bad one: Most
successful fast-food chains do thorough research on possible locations before deciding where the best place is to
sell their fried chicken or hamburgers!

I am definitely not advocating that the church tailor
its ministry on the basis of market research. Rather, I
wish to emphasize that instances of practice do not occur
in a vacuum. They occur in particular settings that provide opportunities for as well as set limits on ministry. It
is most often crucial for us to know how elements of the
setting, far too many and complex to consider here, may
be important for understanding a particular situation.[11] I
emphasize "may be" because not everything in the setting will be important for every situation of ministry
practice. What is relevant obviously depends on the issue
at hand.

There is a temporal setting, not only the setting's
now but also its past, insofar as it continues to impinge
on the present. Likewise, settings have an ecology, both
physical and human, that characterizes the relationships
among individuals, institutions, and their physical environment. Settings also have a demography: the number
of people who make them up, their age, gender, racial

and ethnic characteristics, level of education, income, and occupation. Demography, in turn, plays an important role in helping to shape what might be called the social worlds of individuals and groups: that is, how different people view the world, put their world together, and give meaning to issues and events. For example, in a brilliant analysis of the abortion conflict, Kristin Luker (1984) helps us to understand the social worlds of pro-life and pro-choice activists. She shows how each group "has an internally coherent and mutually shared view of the world that is tacit, never fully articulated, and, most importantly, completely at odds with the world view held by their opponents" (p. 159). And she helpfully relates the opponents' views of the world to their particular demography and social location.

Such understanding can play an important role in pastoral situations where this and similar issues are joined. Church members, clergy included, do not exist apart from other roles, networks, and institutions that both influence our social worlds and also create cross-pressures that pull and tug on our loyalties. Finally, too, we must take into account interpersonal, intragroup, and institutional characteristics of the setting, including their power dynamics.

The point is that these contextual elements are not extraneous, secondary, or unimportant. They are the setting for the church's embodiment in particular times and places, and they too must be part of the reflective leader's conversation with the situation.

Talkback from the Situation

A final foreground resource is talkback from the situation, especially from others who are our partners in ministry. Since the importance of such talkback was examined at some length in chapter 5, I need only do so briefly here. Reflective leadership involves a symmetrical view of authority. The reflective leader treats others in the situation as partners in reflection-in-action, not as recipients of her or his bountiful expertise. Each partner has perspective and expertise to contribute to the reflective conversation with the situation. Rather than residing in the clergy or lay expert, the appropriate response to most situations of practice is discovered between us, in a mutual, interdependent search.

Carl Dudley (1987) tells of a time when as a pastor he was asked, several weeks in advance, to baptize the baby of an out-of-town couple during the Easter Sunday service. He declined to do so, indicating that the Easter season was too busy. He did not know that one of the parents was the granddaughter of a previous clerk of the session. Upon learning of his response, the grandmother precipitated a meeting of the session. Dudley explained his reasons for refusing the request with "theological eloquence," he indicated. "Grandma was brief. She told them that this was her great-granddaughter." The session voted, and they baptized the baby on Easter. About a month later, Dudley was asked to baptize a baby born out of wedlock:

> When the mother came forward I asked the then Clerk of our Session to join us [using] the liturgical language, "Who stands with this family?" Before the Clerk could arrive at the baptismal font, Grandma stood up. With her stood a few friends, and then a few more, and then the whole congregation stood with this mother and child (Dudley 1987, 3).

The incident moved Dudley to preach, several weeks later, about children born in areas of poverty without paternal presence. As a result the congregation was galvanized to respond to the issues of welfare programs. All of this resulted from the talkback of the grandmother, who understood better than he how things were done in that congregation. She helped him to understand in new ways what was occurring and also helped to mobilize the congregation to see their responsibility as "family" and to address an important social issue. Put in the language of reflective practice, he framed the issue of her great-granddaughter's baptism one way; she framed it differently and changed his practice. Furthermore, she also framed the issue of the "family" of the second baby differently. Her talkback played a significant role in his and the congregation's new response.

Talkback is sometimes less direct but no less important. Recall that Davida Crabtree's first efforts at encouraging lay ministry involved responses that were met with little enthusiasm—a form of talkback. The insights she gained in trying to understand what the lack of enthusiasm meant were important in her reframing of the issue. This was true also of John as he too encountered resistance to planning and goal setting as well as to training retreats and workshops. Martha's efforts to respond to the resistance that characterized Alison's talkback were not so successful. Alison's need for control reflects a vision of the church and her role in it that is at odds with Martha's. As a result Martha can acquiesce, or she may be able to find a way to get behind Alison's resistance so that together they can move beyond the impasse. Failing this, she may need to find ways of leading that circumvent Alison's resistance.

The importance of talkback as a resource for reflective leadership is obvious. It does not diminish the need for clergy leadership, nor does it undermine the clergy's authority. Rather, it removes the leader's need to be the sole expert and makes the construction of practice a mutual, interdependent enterprise.

PUTTING IT ALL TOGETHER

Given this rather extensive list of resources out of which the reflective leader constructs his or her practice, one may feel somewhat like the proverbial centipede who is immobilized when he stops to think which foot goes first. One may also wonder where, in the process of constructing practice, is the leading of the Holy Spirit. In concluding this chapter, let me attend briefly to these two questions.

In response to the first, I need only to remind the reader of the *praxis*-based process of reflecting-in-action described in the preceding chapter. It may be helpful to reread the chapter in light of the discussion of resources for practice. Short of that, let me reiterate the broad out-lines of the process. While there is no one best way to construct one's practice—if there were, it would be a form of technical rationality—there is a meta-method, a hermeneutic of practice, involved that can serve us whether we are engaged in meaning definition, commu-nity building, or enabling public ministry. As one en-gages in a reflective conversation, one frames the issue and one's role in it: Is it this, or is it that? One also tries to understand the dynamics of the situation, weighing the importance of this or that factor. In the process one ex-periments with possible responses, listening to the situa-tion's talkback, until an appropriate resolution is found. Throughout the process, the various resources described, background and foreground, will be brought into play. Background resources, which may be more tacit than ex-plicit, are especially important in the way one initially frames issues and one's own role in them. Background resources also often shape which foreground resources are appropriate and how they will be used. Foreground resources help us in understanding the situation's dy-namics and the possible responses open to us. This whole reflective conversation implies a kind of systemic thinking as one seeks to construct responses that are both faithful to the church's identity as the body of Christ and appropriate to the situation at hand. It is not simply *one* thing that must be taken into account but a set of inter-acting factors and resources that must be considered and weighed.

Where does the leading of the Holy Spirit come into

the picture? The answer is not as a kind of deus ex machina to which we turn to avoid the hard discipline of reflecting-in-action or when all else has failed. Nor do we turn to the Holy Spirit after we have done our reflecting-in-action as an afterthought or a bit of divine insurance. By raising the question of the Holy Spirit at this late stage in the discussion, I am leaving myself open to just such criticism. I was, however, quite deliberate in leaving it until last. To be sure, the regular disciplines of prayer and meditation are crucial for the Christian's life. They are essential for nourishing the vision or *habitus* that informs our ministry. They are also essential in preparing us for the acts of discernment that come as one reflects-in-action. Reflecting-in-action is not, therefore, divorced from prayer and meditation. Rather, it is itself a form of prayer as we think systemically, opening ourselves to the full range of resources available to us to construct our responses. It is also a form of prayer as we refuse to force our will on others but join interdependently with them in seeking a faithful response. Above all, it is a form of prayer as we seek to test our practice by the shape of Jesus' ministry in our effort to ensure the church's Christian identity. The very general criteria suggested in chapter 4 provide one such test: Does our practice enable men and women to enter a new relationship with God that gives their lives meaning and purpose? Does it foster a community based on forgiveness, mutuality, and concern for the neighbor? Does it empower members of the community to live as the people of God in the world? I believe that specific instances of practice should be consistent with all three, even if the practice does not directly address one or more of the criteria. These are criteria on which I draw. Others may nuance them differently.

Reflecting-in-action is not easy. It requires discipline and hard work. Even then the responses we construct are almost always less than perfect. Paul reminds us that "now we see in a mirror dimly." We know only "in part." Yet he also reminds us that "with sighs too deep for words," the Spirit intercedes for us. God's Spirit is in the midst of our reflective conversations, assisting our understanding, guiding our use of the resources available to us, prompting the talkback and guiding our quest for responses that are faithful to the Christian story and appropriate within the often complex, messy, dimly lit situations of practice.

8

REPRESENTING THE SACRED AND REFLECTIVE LEADERSHIP

"The rational does not exhaust the human."
—Max Weber

Credat Emptor: Let the buyer trust.

Chapter 2 discussed two penultimate bases of authority: representing the sacred and expertise. Chapters 6 and 7 focused on a way of construing expertise in terms of the kind of reflective leadership that the church needs in the complex world in which it exists today. The expertise dimension of reflective leadership constitutes a kind of meta-method for ministry, a way of thinking theologically about all that one does in ministry. Put differently, it is a method for dealing with the complexity of ministry practice as one seeks to ensure that one's leadership in meaning interpreting, community formation, and supporting public ministry is faithful to the church's calling to be Christ's body under ever-changing circumstances. The expertise involved in reflective leadership, therefore, cuts across the various kinds of special expertise—for example, preaching or pastoral care—that one needs to function with authority as a clergyperson.

If this is so, then what is the relationship to reflective leadership of the other penultimate basis for authority, being a representative of the sacred? Its importance for clergy leadership is underscored in one of the vignettes in chapter 1. Recall the pastor who prided herself on a well-run church but whose lay parishioners, while appreciating her skills, remarked about her lack of spiritual depth. Another way of expressing her problem, as the laity saw it, is to say that she based her authority on expertise but lacked authority as a representative of the sacred. Must the two remain separate? If not, how are they related? These questions are the focus of this final chapter.

Expertise and Representing the Sacred

Earlier, I mentioned the priest in Graham Greene's novel *The Power and the Glory*, who reluctantly agreed to celebrate the Mass for parishioners in the village where he was hiding from the police. In spite of his own loss of faith and moral failures he was, as he said, still able to "put God in their mouths." He continued to represent God in their midst. Certainly only minimal expertise was required or exhibited, yet the people acknowledged his authority.

Or consider another fictional example: Father Mulcahy of television's M*A*S*H. Clearly, Father Mulcahy was quite different from Greene's whiskey priest. He was portrayed as a man of integrity, a deeply caring person, though we know little of his expertise in specific clergy roles. Only infrequently did we hear him preach or see him conducting religious services. Yet unlike many representations of clergy on television or in films, Father Mulcahy ministered with authority. Richard Kirk (1983, 7) has aptly described the basis of Mulcahy's authority:

> In the chaos of incoming wounded Fr. Mulcahy moves as a symbol of the presence of one who

brought order out of the primeval chaos and so established a cosmos at creation. In the midst of the absurdities of the Korean police action he stands as a living sign of one in whom people can place their faith, which includes their doubts, and find a purpose and a meaning for their lives. Amid the horror and tragedy of war he serves as a reminder of the one who is able to bring some good out of the worst of evils, including a crucifixion. As he prays with the dying and ministers the last rites he represents the hope of the resurrection.

"It is not so much what Fr. Mulcahy does," Kirk concludes, "as it is what he represents. His life has a sacramental quality" (p. 8). In this sense, both Father Mulcahy and the whiskey priest, for all his failings, share a common basis for their authority.

These two examples represent a sacramental view of ministry from a high church or Catholic perspective. The whiskey priest is an extreme example of what earlier was referred to as authority of office, while Father Mulcahy combines his sacramental office with personal qualities that contribute to his authority. But what of authority based on representing the sacred in the more low church traditions, where authority of office sometimes counts for less or is not interpreted in sacramental terms? Consider one further example, this one from Annie Dillard's account of a church service in her book *Holy the Firm* (1977, 57–59). She describes attending a small Congregational church where twenty in attendance is a big Sunday. The minister, who "wears a white shirt," is "a man [who] knows God":

> Once, in the middle of the long pastoral prayer of intercession for the whole world—for the gift of wisdom to its leaders, for hope and mercy to the grieving and pained, succor to the oppressed, and God's grace to all—in the middle of this he stopped,

and burst out, "Lord, we bring you these same peti-
tions every week." After a shocked pause, he continued reading the prayer. Because of this, I like him
very much.

Dillard continues with a description of the rather prosaic
church service and the people, and she contrasts them
with what she calls "the higher Christian churches" who
"come at God with an unwarranted air of professionalism, with authority and pomp, as though they knew
what they were doing":

> In the high churches they saunter through the lit-
> urgy like Mohawks along a strand of scaffolding
> who have long since forgotten their danger. If God
> were to blast such a service to bits, the congregation
> would be, I believe, genuinely shocked. But in the
> low churches you expect it any minute (p. 59).

Both in the demeanor of the minister and the expectations of the people, the presence of the sacred is felt or
clearly anticipated.

Is the import of these examples that expertise really
matters little, that if others grant authority to clergy they
do so on the basis of their representative or sacramental
character, because their presence symbolizes God's presence in the midst of life? One could, perhaps, draw such
a conclusion. It is true that many of us who are clergy
have bumbled along inexpertly; yet, by God's grace, we
have been a blessing to people because of the One whom
we represent. But are we satisfied with this as an adequate basis for clergy leadership?

Having argued for expertise, especially that of reflective practice, as one of the bases of clergy authority, I
obviously believe it to be of great importance. While it
has become fashionable to criticize the professional
model of ministry (e.g., Holmes 1971; Hauerwas and
Willimon 1989), most of us want competence in those
who lead the church or minister to us in times of need,

even as we want competent physicians to treat our illnesses and competent lawyers to advise and assist us in legal matters. By itself, however, expertise is incomplete, even as being a representative of the sacred is incomplete without expertise. The two are not really opposed; rather, they are complementary.

Expertise is the doing or instrumental facet of reflective leadership; sacramental presence describes its being or expressive character. The two belong together and cannot be separated without damaging the church's witness. Thomas Long (1985) makes this point vividly by drawing on the story of Moses and Aaron: Moses with his profound relationship to the mystery of God, Aaron without the vision but with the gifts of public speaking which Moses lacked. Their gifts were complementary. All went well so long as they held them together. But while Moses, the "Vision," was on the mountaintop, Aaron, the "Expert," was in the valley under pressure from the people to point God out. As Long puts it vividly:

> Finally Aaron yields and does what ministerial practice always does when it is cut off from its vision of the active presence of God; he fashions a god for them from the materials at hand. Since there is no Mystery, there is only mechanical method (p. 1).

Findings from a suggestive exploratory study by John Fletcher (1975) highlight the complementarity. He asked a sample of laity to describe the factors affecting their relationships with clergy. The attribute that his respondents most often mentioned is what he came to call "religious authenticity." Laity described authentic clergy variously as "having head and heart together," as reflected in the person who "lives the gospel," or as evident in one who is both "a man of God and a man of the world." The laity valued the clergy's expertise, but the being dimension, their religious authenticity, made possible deep personal bonds without which expertise mattered little.

What is the peculiar contribution of sacramental presence to the reflective leader's ministry practice? In the preceding chapter, I noted one contribution: to the pastor's basic theological vision or her *habitus*, to use Edward Farley's term. While one's *habitus* informs one's expertise, it also reflects a person's fundamental relationship with God and thus is also related to one's authority as a representative of the sacred. Here I simply remind the reader of the important contribution *habitus* makes through shaping and directing one's ministry practice.

In the following sections, I explore two further implications of the clergy's status as representative of the sacred for reflective leadership. The first is the role that being a symbol of God's presence plays in clergy practice, regardless of the clergy's character or personal spirituality. The second is the relationship of sacramental presence to priestly character, especially to the trust relationship—the fiduciary bond—that exists between pastor and laity in pastoral relationships. These are closely related issues, but they warrant separate treatment. They and the clergy's *habitus* are grounded in the call to ministry, which is considered in the final section of the chapter.

Before pursuing these two implications, however, it is important to reiterate a fundamental theological conviction about the church which was discussed more fully in chapter 3: the priesthood of all Christians. More accurately, it is the priesthood of the *community of Christians* that continues to embody the ministry of Jesus. As our "high priest," Jesus, crucified and risen, fully incarnates God's power and purposes in our midst. In baptism all of us, clergy and laity alike, are incorporated into his body and become the embodiment of his continuing sacramental presence in the world.[1] This is the basis of the priesthood into which God calls all Christians. It is not clergy per se who are the priests. Indeed, it is the restriction of priesthood (and sacramental presence) to clergy that has been so pernicious in the history of clergy-laity relationships. The whole people of God in their gathered and scattered life are priests. All Christians are sacramental persons. This is especially true of the corporate embodiment of the church in congregations and other communal forms. If clergy are set apart as somehow special, it is only because they are first among equals. Their specialness is not ontological but functional: They have a distinctive leadership role to play in and on behalf of the community.

So, in last analysis it is the church, not the clergy, that represents the mystery of God in the midst of life. But as first among equals in this priestly community, clergy are the ones most fully identified with God's mystery. They are representative persons, institutionalized symbols of God's presence. Like it or not, those of us who are clergy bring more than our humanity and our expertise to our ministry practice. By our presence, we represent "the mystery that surrounds our life," to use Urban Holmes' words that were cited in chapter 2. The question is not how one escapes this burden—for it clearly can be a burden—but how one understands and uses it responsibly as a gift that enhances one's capacity to lead.

Symbolizing God's Presence

Consider first the contribution that this representative status—whether interpreted in high or low church terms—makes in the various roles in which clergy engage. In these roles in which one attempts to function as a reflective leader, being a symbol of God's presence operates on at least two levels, manifest and latent.

At a more manifest level it adds, for want of a better way to express it, sacred weight to a clergy person's expertise in various roles. Representing the One who gives meaning and purpose to life lends heightened seriousness to what we say or do in our practice of ministry. In meaning interpretation, for example—preaching, liturgical leadership, pastoral counseling, teaching—it is not just Joe or Jane Doe giving an opinion. He or she represents God. The vestments or distinctive clothing that many wear and the Bible that some hold while preaching are visible reminders of the representative role in which the clergy person is engaged. Sometimes, unfortunately, some have concluded that a tombstone voice also adds sacred weight to their preaching and prayers. In most cases, if my experience is any indication, it has the opposite effect!

In my conversation with John, the Lutheran pastor whom we met in the preceding chapter, he described how his congregation typically accepts his preaching and teaching with little questioning because there is a "sacramental aura," as he puts it, involved in the pastor's role as interpreter of the Word. "For Lutherans," he noted, "preaching, like the Eucharist, invokes the real presence of Christ. It's not just a homily. The vestments and everything else that goes with the role suggest this." For these reasons, John feels a considerable burden of responsibility to interpret the Word faithfully and with integrity. In such fashion he melds authority as a sacramental person with authority based on expertise.

Similarly, to take another example, the fact that clergy represent the sacred and function in the context of the church creates a dynamic for *pastoral* counseling different from that of the psychotherapist's couch. The expertise each needs may be similar in many respects, but the role and context differ in significant ways and change the authority dynamics.[2]

When laity do question a pastor's teaching or counsel, it often involves much more pain than other forms of disagreement. This was illustrated in an incident from another television situation comedy, "Designing Women." The episode, rare for commercial television, focused on the ordination of women. One of the characters, Charlene, is a Southern Baptist layperson who harbored an unfulfilled dream as a teenager of becoming a pastor. In the episode, she becomes deeply troubled by her pastor's strong opposition to ordaining women. After a group discussion where he reiterates his opposition, she goes to him in distress to resign her membership in the congregation. She tells him that she has trusted him to interpret God's Word, but she no longer finds that she can do so—not if his teaching about ministry excludes both her and half of the human race. The pastor, visibly surprised and disturbed by her decision, tries to dissuade her. He tells her that just because the two of them don't agree doesn't mean that she has to leave the congregation or that they cannot continue as friends. "But," Charlene replies with deep feeling, "you're not just my friend. You're my pastor!" That he spoke as God's representative made him more than a friend, and it increased the difficulty and pain of disagreement.

Being perceived as a representative of the sacred can also be a blessing. Which of us has not been surprised to find that the presence of the One whom we represent has compensated for our halting, inadequate words in the face of a parishioner's suffering or death? As a pastor, I often found myself at loss for appropriate words when ministering to a grieving family. I would sometimes simply sit with them in silence, unwilling to express what felt to me to be empty clichés yet unable to say anything that seemed meaningful in the face of their loss. To my surprise, they would thank me for the comfort that I brought them. Their gratitude was not simply for the comfort of a friend's presence. Rather, it was for the comfort of the One whom I as pastor symbolized. I was with them as bearer of the mystery of God on behalf of the priestly community.

A seminarian describes a similar experience with remarkable insight as she reflected on her first funeral as a student pastor in a small congregation:

> A member of the congregation died and I was to have his funeral. I met with the family in their home

and heard their cries of disbelief: "Why Bill?" "He
had so much to live for." "How am I going to get on
without him?" I joined silently in their cries, "Why
me, God?"

There I was at the time of the service, scared stiff,
never having done a funeral before, feeling alone.
We were all treading through foggy, unfamiliar
ground. I felt as if my senses had left me, blind and
groping for the right words and actions. And yet it
was me, shaking, blind, nearly unable to speak in
the face of such pain and confusion, it is me to
whom they turned for support, for good news in
this darkness. I was the one among the believers
gathered who was expected to stand in that place
between their pain and the hope that is our faith. I
felt the tension even in what I was wearing, the pull
between the black robe and the cotton dress beneath. But in that gathering I felt the support of
believers not only in that congregation of all those
who had gone before. There in our midst was
Christ, speaking through all of us, through even me,
words of assurance—proclaiming the hope and joy-
ous news of the gospel to all who had assembled. In
that service we were all given the ability to go on
assured anew of God's grace. We were able to feel
the pain and yet continue because of our faith and
the renewing presence of the Spirit working in our
lives (cited in Dudley and Hilgert 1987, 98).

The student discovered the sacramental presence of
Christ in the community of believers, and she also discovered the power of her own priestly role as the primary representative of that community, in spite of her
feeling that she lacked the competence to cope with the
situation. Her black robe covered her cotton dress and
helped symbolically to point to the Other whom she and
the community represented. Let the reader also note that,

besides illustrating the power of the symbolic role that clergy play, her account is a helpful example of how one learns from reflecting on one's ministry practice in a way that enhances future practice.

The representative role that clergy play extends beyond the gathered community to the public ministry of the church. While I have emphasized that in public life it is the laity who are the primary ministers and priests, the clergy's symbolic status also is operative in the public arena. As noted in chapter 4, when my colleagues and I (McKinney, Roozen, and Carroll 1983) interviewed community leaders about the role of religion in public life, the leaders often identified that role with clergy. While it was important for congregations collectively and lay Christians individually to be involved in public ministry, community leaders took special note of clergy involvement. Unless ministers, priests, or rabbis were present and visible in community affairs, the interviewees often considered religion to be absent. The clergy's presence lent symbolic weight to religion's public presence. I have difficulty with the leaders' perspective if they restrict religion's or God's presence only to the presence and activity of clergy. That is to deny the priesthood of all Christians. Yet I can understand their perspective from a phenomenological perspective. The leaders are acknowledging the distinctive representative role that clergy play, even if their role might more accurately be understood as first among equals in the priestly community through which God is present.

Beyond the manifest contribution that the pastor's sacramental status as representing God's presence makes, there is also a more latent one. It is not simply that their symbolic role gives sacred weight or sacred presence to what clergy do or say, sometimes in spite of their inadequacies. There are also the phenomena, that I confess not fully to understand, of projection and transference. At the most elemental level, they are seen in the small child's confusing the pastor with God. Most clergy have experienced this identification when making a pastoral call: "Mom, God's at the door!" In a more complex way, however, a similar identification occurs with adults. Clergy become the objects onto which others project their deepest feelings, unresolved questions, and hopes about God. By symbolizing the sacred in the midst of life clergy make God, who seems often far and hidden, near to the particularity of human needs. While clergy especially are the objects of projection and transference, these processes are, to reiterate, another way of describing the role of the whole people of God as a priestly community. The *church's* task, not just that of the clergy, is to represent the nearness of God to the particularity of human need. Nonetheless, clergy, as first among equals, are vulnerable in a special way to being identified with the sacred and thus become objects of transference and projection. Resist it though we may, such processes occur and are often healthy. They make it possible for others to deal with God face-to-face, so to speak. As Loren Mead (1976, 4) has described it, "insofar as I am perceived to be a pastor, that person facing me lays important, sometimes very tender, defensive or fearful projections upon me, not because of who I am but because of an authority he or she imputes to me as a bearer of a mystery. This is not something I cause to happen or even am aware of most of the time."

Reflecting again on the incident from "Designing Women," another reason Charlene could not be content with her pastor's interpretation of their disagreement as one between friends was because she had projected onto him her deepest hopes and feelings about God. The pastor's rejection of women's ordination, and therefore also of her, was so painful because it felt as if she were being rejected by God. Fortunately, her experience of God was not limited to God's symbolic presence in that particular pastor.

Transference and projection are often helpful, necessary experiences. They enable a person to clarify his or her thoughts, feelings, and perplexities about God and God's purposes. They help a person break through defenses and acknowledge dependence not on the clergy but on God. They make it possible for a person to "become as a little child," a necessity, as Jesus said, for entering the kingdom of heaven (see Matthew 18:3).[3] At the same time, they can also create an unhealthy dependence on the pastor (or on the church community), a dependence and depth of trust that leaves the person extremely vulnerable to exploitation. We are painfully aware of the apparently growing incidence of sexual abuse within the pastoral relationship or of clergy involvement in pederasty. Transference and projection create the climate for such vulnerability in the pastoral relationship. Whether such incidents are in fact more frequent now than earlier or simply more openly publicized is almost impossible to say. They nevertheless raise serious issues for clergy and for other professions as well. I will return to them in the next section, where I consider the implications of the clergy's sacramental status for trust in pastor-parishioner relationships.

To sum up, the *being* of clergy—being a symbol of God's presence in the midst of life—is not antithetical to expertise in reflective leadership. Being a symbol of God's presence contributes to clergy authority by lending sacred weight or seriousness to what clergy say and do in their various roles. It also contributes latently as clergy represent the nearness of God to the particularity of human needs. This makes healthy—and sometimes unhealthy—transference possible. Because of this special representative role and its capacity for abuse, it is a gift to be nourished and used responsibly.

Let us note that clergy are not alone among professionals in representing the mystery that surrounds life. Physicians also deal in sacred matters, issues of life and death. Though we value their medical expertise, we also frequently look to them for something more, especially when our very existence is at stake. In a remarkable es-

say, the literary critic Anatole Broyard (1990) described
his feelings about the physicians he encountered as he
dealt with cancer: "I would like a doctor who is not only
a talented physician but a bit of a metaphysician too,
someone who can treat body and soul." He described
how his father,

> who was an old fashioned Southern anti-Semite, in-
> sisted on a Jewish doctor when he developed cancer
> of the bladder. A Jewish doctor, he argued, had
> been bred to medicine. In my father's biblical con-
> ception, a Jew's life was a story of study, repair and
> reform. A Jewish doctor knew what survival was
> worth, because he had to fight for his. Obliged to
> treat life as a business as well as a pleasure, Jews
> drove hard bargains. To lose a patient was bad busi-
> ness. In his heart, I think my father believed that a
> Jewish doctor was closer to God and could use that
> connection to "Jew down" death.

As with John Fletcher's description of religiously authentic clergy, Broyard is in touch with a spiritual, priestly
dimension of the physician's role. It is a dimension that
we sometimes recognize by its absence in particular doctors but celebrate when we experience it in others.

SACRAMENTAL PRESENCE AND TRUST

The clergy's symbolic status as representatives of
the sacred has an additional implication for exercising
authority. It has to do with trustworthiness. Clergy are
called to deal with people in the deepest moments of
their lives. People come to them in times of high vulnerability. Those who come need to be able to trust that their
vulnerability will not be exploited. It is not enough that I
have confidence in my pastor's expertise, though I clearly
expect her to be competent. I also need to trust that she
will exercise a fiduciary responsibility towards me, that

she will act in my best interests, or that she will act in the best interests of the congregation in its struggle to be faithful to the gospel.

Our need to trust the pastor and, conversely, the pastor's obligation to honor that trust is the significance of the Latin phrase *credat emptor*. It means "let the buyer believe" or "let the buyer trust." It stands in sharp contrast to the more familiar *caveat emptor*, "let the buyer beware," often used as a motto for the exchange of goods in the marketplace. The sociologist Everett Hughes (1968, 657) once suggested that we might consider *credat emptor* as a motto for the professions generally. "The client," said Hughes, "is to trust the professional; he must tell him all secrets which bear upon the affairs in hand. He must trust his judgment and skill." "Trust me," the slick automobile salesperson oozes in a popular television commercial, but the buyer knows that *caveat emptor* is the operative norm.[4] "Trust me," the professional asks, and the client or parishioner complies on the basis of *credat emptor*. The professional has a fiduciary responsibility in the relationship to act in the best interests of the client's and public's welfare. The basis for trust of professionals generally is an important one that has evoked considerable discussion (e.g., Barber 1983, 131ff.). Here, however, I want to focus especially on trust in clergy-laity relationships.

What is the basis of one's trust of his or her pastor? As with our willingness to grant authority generally, our trust is based in part on our belief that he or she has the competence to provide the leadership the church needs or to help me address my particular needs. But more than an expectation of competence is involved. Expectations about the pastor's character are also at issue.

Let me illustrate: Some years ago, my wife and I were driving to my college reunion in South Carolina. Just as we arrived in the city where the reunion was being held, our car broke down. We pulled into a service station to see if it could be repaired. It could not, at least not that evening, and it was unsafe to drive it farther. As we debated options for reaching the reunion site, a stranger said, "Why don't you take my car? I'll get a ride home, and you can return it here to the station tomorrow." While we were flabbergasted by his generous offer, we declined to keep his car. We did, however, accept a ride to the reunion site. I asked him why he would trust a total stranger with his car. He replied that he was a coach at my alma mater, and he assumed that any Wofford College graduate was trustworthy. (Indeed, when I was a student there, being a "Wofford gentleman"—it was an all-male school then—was an important part of the normative culture.) While the coach may be faulted for extreme naivete, there is some similarity to his willingness to trust me and a parishioner's willingness to trust her pastor or priest. In the coach's mind, being a Wofford graduate symbolized something about character that made even a total stranger trustworthy. Being a representative of the sacred has a similar power. In spite of clergy moral and spiritual failures that have violated the fiduciary bond, others are willing to trust clergy because they believe that, as a representative of the sacred, the pastor or priest is worthy of such trust. Their trust is based on expectations about the character of the One whom clergy represent. Because one believes that God is trustworthy, so also does one expect the pastor to be trustworthy. Because one believes that God is just, one expects fairness from the pastor. Because one believes that God is truth, one expects truth telling from the pastor. Because one believes that God cares so deeply for humankind that, in Christ, God plumbed the depths of human life, so also does one expect empathy, compassion, and care from the pastor. Because one believes that the God whom one knows in Jesus will never act to violate the good of the creation, which includes one's own good, one expects that the priest or pastor will also act with his or her good and that of the community in view.

Of course, the reverse may also be true. Rather than

deducing that clergy will be trustworthy from our convictions about God, many times we begin more inductively. We may be helped to trust God more fully because we experience God's presence in the trustworthiness, fairness, compassion, care, and truth telling of others, including pastors and priests. Indeed, I suspect that this inductive way of proceeding may be as common as the more deductive approach. But it is possible because of the priestly, symbolic character of the people of God generally and of the clergy in particular. Either way underscores the significance of the fiduciary bond in pastoral relationships.[5]

When such qualities characterize the bond between congregations and their pastor or priest, they contribute in important ways to his or her capacity to function as a reflective leader. A willingness to make one's self vulnerable, to show empathy, to express care and compassion, to tell the truth, to be just, to seek the good of the individual or that of the community—such qualities create a kind of "mystical geography"[6] that bonds the pastor and parishioner in a common relational turf. They help pastoral relationships to be healing, redemptive, and liberating. They call forth the gifts and reflective capacities of others in the relationship. Belgian sociologist Lillian Voye (1989) tells of observing a number of Christian communities that formed outside the structures of the church, to some extent similar to the base communities of Latin America. Some of them met without benefit of clergy, but others had priests who met with them in leadership roles. In one group, the members asked the priest to leave. A member commented on the dismissal: "The priest was the one who *knew*; then we told him that he didn't suit us. Now we have a new one (he hasn't come by way of the hierarchy) and *we feel the difference: he dares to speak about himself; it's richer for the group than if he acted as the one who knows and concludes*" (p. 10, emphasis supplied). In a manner similar to the group's feelings about the first priest, a friend once reflected his keen

disappointment with the new minister who had been appointed to his church: "He's quite professional, he knows
a lot, his sermons seem carefully prepared and are deliv-
ered with polish; but when it comes to personal and pastoral relationships, he's a cold fish! I just don't trust him."
The mystical geography was absent.

Recognizing the importance of the relational bond
between physicians and patients, some medical schools
are attempting to teach what they call "the connexional
dimension of medical care" (Suchman and Matthews
1988; Matthews, Suchman, and Branch n.d.). This dimension expands the dominant medical model of empiri-
cal science by adding what the authors refer to as
"transpersonal" or "spiritual" qualities. At times, they
even speak of the "priestly" character of the physician's
role. They describe this connexional dimension as involving "listening beneath the surface of the patient's complaints," "demonstrating personal concern," "simply
being there with a patient," and so forth. After summarizing a number of connexional experiences with patients, they conclude:

> Through understanding, patience, and special mo-
> ments of rapport, the foundation of a mutually re-
> warding long-term relationship of caring and trust
> can be laid. This type of doctor-patient relationship
> can be healing. In fact, the major therapeutic vehicle
> in the cases described . . . was not the technology,
> or the pharmaceuticals, but the relationship itself.
> When the physician makes an effort to understand
> the patient's world, however unusual or even bi-
> zarre, when he or she makes a telephone call out of
> "the blue," or performs an act of friendship well
> beyond the call of ordinary duty, or even just listens
> attentively to what troubles the patient, he or she
> demonstrates dedication and caring which the pa-
> tient perceives as being therapeutic . . . The doctor-
> patient relationship can be healing when the patient

trusts the physician, shares burdens and sufferings, feels accepted and secure in the relationship, and can perceive through this relationship that his or her burdens and sufferings are unique yet simultaneously part of broad human experience (Matthews, Suchman, and Branch n.d., 26).

The connexional dimension, whether in medicine or ministry, does not diminish the importance of expertise. Rather, it creates the space, the fiduciary bond, "the mystical geography," in which one's expertise can have its greatest effect. For the pastor or priest—and perhaps also less obviously for the physician—it is a part of what it means to represent the sacred in the midst of life.

REPRESENTING THE SACRED AND CALLING

All this may seem to imply that representing the sacred requires that clergy—perhaps physicians and other professionals as well—need to be moral and spiritual giants. This, however, is not the case. Let me try to unpack the issue by reference to the important distinction between office and person introduced in chapter 2.

It is not because priests or pastors are *necessarily*, on a personal level, any more holy, caring, or closer to God than lay Christians that their roles have sacred weight or that they are worthy of trust. All Christians are called to holiness even as all of us live by grace as redeemed sinners. Beyond this, however, the clergy *office* or *role* provides added help. The clergy role contains normative expectations about what it means to be representatives of the sacred, including being trustworthy. Though they vary by denominational tradition and local culture, these expectations are built in to the role. Most clergy internalize these expectations over time, and they become part of their pastoral identity. Even when internalization is not complete, these expectations function as a kind of "schoolmaster" or "custodian" (to use Paul's words about the role of the law; see Galatians 3:24). Clergy who in their inner motivations are not always caring or altruistic are nevertheless often of genuine help to parishioners and their congregations. They fulfill the fiduciary obligations of the clergy *role* even when their personal motivation flags.[7]

Why is this distinction between office or role and person important? It emphasizes that the fiduciary obligation is, first of all, an institutional expectation of the office of priest or pastor, not one that rests on the subjective state of the person. A male pastor may have sexual fantasies about a female counselee, but his internalized role expectations are strong enough that he sublimates those fantasies and uses his counseling expertise to help her. A pastor may be much more invested in advancing her career than in whether her congregation's leaders find a way to respond to a racially changing neighborhood. But role expectations that she will provide leadership overcome her inertia. In doing so, she exercises fiduciary responsibility towards them even when she has little inner motivation to do so—as Graham Greene's whiskey priest does when he reluctantly agrees to celebrate the sacrament. This structural dimension of the clergy office helps a pastor or priest to keep faith with his or her calling, to keep on keeping on in those dark nights of the soul when the inner motives flag or when it appears that God is dead or at least gone on a journey.

Having said this, however, I do not wish to diminish the significance of the pastor's inner being, his or her personal religious authenticity—whether or not we believe (as I do not) in an indelible priestly character that one receives in ordination. Even if not impossible, it is exceedingly difficult to symbolize God's trustworthiness in midst of life if one is not also a participant in that reality. It is difficult to lead others to a vision of God's *shalom* if one's own vision is not regularly restored at one's own equivalent of the pool of Siloam (see John 9). Whatever else Gilbert Tennent may have meant when he argued for a converted ministry, he was affirming the critical importance of the pastor's own existential knowledge of God's amazing grace. Father Mulcahy was trusted not solely because of his priestly office. His personal religious authenticity in the conduct of that office also shone through. That seems also the case for the Congregational minister whom Annie Dillard described with such appreciation: He was "a man who knows God."

Such existential knowledge reflects one's call to ministry, both the call to be a Christian that comes to laity and clergy alike and the more specific call to enter ordained ministry that comes to some. The latter includes what some have referred to as a *churchly call*, a recognition by a church body that one has the requisite gifts for ministry, and a *secret call*, a deep inner conviction that one is called to ordained ministry.[8] The secret call comes in an encounter with God in the depths of one's being. It may be a dramatic, numinous experience such as that of Jacob in his dream, Moses on the mountaintop, Isaiah in the temple, or Paul on the Damascus road, or instead it may be a more gradual sense of awakening to a vocation. This encounter—dramatic or gradual—is at the heart of the *habitus*, the vision of Christian faith and life that shapes one's being and one's ministry practice. It lies behind the quality of religious authenticity that makes representing the sacred more than a matter of external office: One's *person* as well as one's office symbolizes God's presence; one *is* trustworthy and not simply presumed to be so *ex officio*.

Even as one's call from God is related to one's authority as representative of the sacred, so also is it related to one's expertise as a professional, as noted earlier. Some have maintained that the professional model of ministry, with its emphasis on expertise, is antithetical to a ministry grounded in an experience of God's call. This is simply not so. Both are essential as distinct but complementary elements of a ministry that is both faithful and effective. As James Gustafson (1982, 514) has put it so well:

> A "calling" without professionalization [expertise] is bumbling, ineffective, and even dangerous. A profession without a calling, however, has no taps of moral and human rootage to keep motivation alive, to keep human sensitivities and sensibilities alert, and to nourish a proper sense of self-fulfillment. Nor does a profession without a calling easily envision the larger ends and purposes of human good that our individual efforts can serve.

It is when a lively sense of calling undergirds and fuses the expertise of reflective leadership with sacramental presence that we experience a renewal of our authority as ordained leaders in the church—an authority that builds up the body of Christ and empowers it to continue Christ's ministry in the world. It is not inconceivable that some, perhaps with astonishment, will say of clergy who learn to lead reflectively what they said of Jesus: "He [or she] taught them as one who had authority, and not as the scribes!"

NOTES

Chapter 1
As One Without Authority?

1. In his book *American Evangelicalism: Conservative Religion and the Quandary of Modernity* (1983, 73ff.), Hunter describes what he calls the "new style evangelical," who has gone through a "domestication of belief" to make it less objectionable and more relevant to the needs and perspectives of modern men and women. Such efforts at accommodation are in large measure at the root of the current conflict between hard-line fundamentalists and moderates within the Southern Baptist Convention.

2. Denominations that have been considered mainline—a railroad metaphor—are those that have been located near the center of American culture and include, among others, Episcopalians, Presbyterians, Congregationalists (now the United Church of Christ), Methodists, Baptists, and, more recently, Lutherans. These denominations have functioned in the past as an unofficial, de facto religious establishment. For a helpful analysis of mainline Protestantism, see Roof and McKinney (1987).

3. See, for example, Letty Russell (1979, 1987) and Hahn (1985).

Chapter 2
Authority Is Not a Four-Letter Word

1. Quoted in Sweet (1982, 721).

2. For extended discussion of theories of authority see, for example, Nisbet (1966), Lukes (1978), and Sennett (1980).

3. Following the 1954 Supreme Court decision that struck down the "separate but equal" doctrine in public education, most Protestant denominations in the South passed nonbinding resolutions about the decision, which the large majority of congregations and individual members ignored. The Catholic Church, however, strongly supported the decision and instructed its priests to move to integrate their parishes. They were told that they could use the power of excommunication for recalcitrant parishioners. As one priest said to me, "That is a heavy ax to hold over a person's head." How much effect it had on individual Catholic behavior, I do not know. I suspect much less so than in the past.

4. The Archbishop of the Diocese of Hartford, Connecticut, announced publicly that he had surrendered his Democratic registration because of the Democratic Party's endorsement of a pro-abortion position in their 1988 election platform. He went to great lengths, however, to indicate that his decision, while based on the Church's teachings, was a personal one and not an official recommendation from his teaching office that other Catholics follow his lead. Nevertheless, as *The Hartford Courant* (August 26, 1988) pointed out, there was the strong likelihood that his action would be interpreted as a form of interference in the governmental process and used in the suit being brought against the Church by an abortion rights group.

5. It is true, however, that Weber was extremely pessimistic about modern society because he feared that the spirit of religious asceticism—the charismatic foundation of Western society introduced by the Hebrew prophets and the Protestant ethic—was no longer necessary as the legitimating principle of modern bureaucratic organization (Weber 1958a, 181–182).

6. If it is legitimate to push Weber's view of charisma this far, as I believe it is, then there is a convergence between Weber's view of charisma and Durkheim's (1915) view of the

sacred, as both Parsons (1937) and Nisbet (1966) suggest. A basic difference, however, is Weber's interest in charisma as a source of change while Durkheim concentrated on charisma as a source of stability and order.

7. An excellent discussion of types of religious leaders and bases for authority can be found in Wach (1944, 331–374). See also Weber (1963).

8. In this section, I draw from two previously published essays (Carroll 1981, 1986).

9. See O'Dea's (1966) important discussion, "Dilemmas of Institutionalization." For a critique and reinterpretation of the doctrine of apostolic succession from a Catholic perspective, see Schillebeeckx (1985).

10. Weber's discussion of the differences between prophets and priests echoes the difference between evangelical and sacramental-liturgical understandings of the authority as representative of the sacred. For Weber (1963, 46), "the personal call is the decisive element distinguishing the prophet from the priest. The latter lays claim to authority by virtue of his service in a sacred tradition, while the prophet's claim is based on personal revelation and charisma."

Chapter 3
The Relational Dimensions of Authority

1. See, for example, Schweizer (1961), Shütz (1975), Cooke (1975), Meeks (1983), Schillebeeckx (1985), and Dudley and Hilgert (1987).

2. Of the three historians mentioned, Harlan takes issue with Schmotter and Youngs (and others who share their perspective) as overstating clergy-laity conflict. He believes that they uncritically adopted a neoprogressive interpretive framework in which a clerical oligarchy is set over against a populist laity, with the latter finally triumphing in the aftermath of the Great Awakening (Harlan 1980, 39). Harlan does not deny the pretensions of some clergy or the concern of clergy over their changing status, but he argues (persuasively, in my opinion) that clergy dominance was not as great as others have maintained and that there were a number of prominent clergy who fought against clerical pretension.

3. In Connecticut, the Saybrook Platform of 1708 gave much greater centralized authority to countywide consociations or church councils made up of representatives from congregations than did Massachusetts' Cambridge Platform of 1648. The Connecticut councils, however, were not clergy associations but consisted of both clergy and laity, with the probability that laity may have outnumbered clergy.

4. See also Calhoun (1965). For parallel developments in England, see Anthony Russell (1980). With a somewhat different purpose, King (1981) has traced the history of struggles over authority within American Methodism. These include authority struggles between bishops and clergy as well as between clergy and laity.

5. See, for example, Hadden's (1969) discussion of clergy-laity conflicts over social activism, or Hoge's (1989) analysis of laity-clergy conflicts over priorities in the United Presbyterian Church.

6. See also Hahn (1985) for a very clear and helpful discussion of a church in which symmetrical relationships are the norm. Hahn's contrast between "open" and "closed" models of the church is similar to my contrast between asymmetrical and symmetrical authority relationships.

Chapter 4
Authority and Ecclesiology

1. Kelsey (1975) uses the term in describing how scripture functions normatively for theology. Speaking of judging theological proposals, Kelsey says that biblical texts are not normative because they provide the source from which the proposals are derived. Rather, "it is the *patterns* in scripture, not its 'content,' that make it normative for theology." The patterns are the basis for judging the Christian aptness of a theological proposal.

2. Reed (1978) has drawn on post-Freudian psychological theory to interpret the church in a somewhat similar fashion. He views the church's primary task as that of helping individuals to "regress to extra-dependence," especially in the church's worship. Such regression is not an end in itself but

enables the worshiper to experience renewal and return to his or her daily life in an autonomous or intradependent mode.

3. The statement was made by William Farley at a meeting of the Board of Trustees of Hartford Seminary, September 14, 1988.

Chapter 5
The Central Tasks of Leadership in the Church

1. An earlier version of this chapter appeared in Dudley, Carroll, and Wind (1991).

2. For an extended discussion of cognitive dissonance in relation to the first Christians, see Gager (1975) and Dudley and Hilgert (1987).

3. This has regularly been the case in surveys that Hartford Seminary's Center for Social and Religious Research has assisted parishes to undertake using our Parish Profile Inventory.

4. It was of some interest, however, to note that the parish administrator image was slightly more likely to be affirmed by D.Min. graduates than by clergy who had not enrolled in D.Min. programs. Many D.Min. programs have given considerable attention to organizational development theory and methods as applicable to parish ministry.

5. This example comes from a D.Min. project report (Crabtree 1988), which has subsequently been published as a book (Crabtree 1989).

Chapter 6
Leading with Authority: The Dynamics of Reflective Leadership

1. See, for example, Hough and Cobb (1985).

2. See Farley (1983) for a critique of these assumptions, which reflect what he calls the "clerical paradigm."

3. Harry Stout, who spent a number of years studying preaching in colonial New England (Stout 1986), recently "shadowed" a contemporary New England pastor in the Congregational tradition to observe how he went about sermon preparation and delivery. Much of what he discovered about

the process bore striking resemblance to early New England preaching (Stout 1987). From my perspective, it also exhibits much of the character of reflective practice.

4. In using the method, one selects from ministry practice a challenging incident or interaction for analysis. He or she then begins the case with a few paragraphs describing the purpose of their involvement in the interaction or intervention, the setting, the people involved, and any other important information about the situation. Next, one describes what the strategies were: What were specific objectives? How did he or she intend to achieve them? Why these particular goals and strategies?

Particularly helpful is the next step: writing several pages of the dialogue that actually occurred in the incident or interaction. In this step, the author separates the page with a vertical line. On the right side of the line, one tries to capture the essence of the dialogue, especially the most important segments of it. On the left side, one tries to recall what was going on in his or her mind while each person in the dialogue, including him or herself, was speaking.

Finally, the author rereads and reflects on the case, describing the underlying assumptions that one thinks she or he held about effective action. The author also tries to reflect on the basis for these assumptions: What is it in his or her personal story or approach to ministry that has led to these assumptions?

While the exercise itself can increase self-awareness, even in the absence of trusted colleagues, it can be especially beneficial when one's colleagues join in probing the case. Often they can help one become much more aware of the way one's personal narrative and characteristic ways of framing one's role contribute to or hinder the realization of one's objectives.

Chapter 7

The Structure of Reflective Leadership

1. The distinction between objectivist and constructionist ways of knowing has a long philosophical and theological heritage. Immanuel Kant's distinction between "pure" and "practical" reason and Martin Buber's distinction between "I-It" and "I-Thou" relationships are examples. Similarly, H. Richard Niebuhr (1941) distinguished between "outer" and "inner"

approaches to history: the former objectivist, the other much more constructionist in the intimate relation that it implies between knower and known. More recently, cognitive psychologists have used similar distinctions in contrasting dualist (objectivist) with critical (constructionist) ways of thinking (Kurfiss 1988).

2. In an opposite direction, some biblical scholars have sought objectivity through using linguistic and historical-critical methods to get at the objective truth of scripture—for example, the Jesus of history as contrasted with the Christ of faith.

3. These two sets of elements are my way of trying to describe resources for reflective leadership. A similar approach, using three elements (tradition, experience, and culture), has been put forward by James D. and Evelyn Eaton Whitehead in their book *Method in Ministry* (1981). I have been much helped by their discussion and also by Browning's (1983) discussion of elements of practical theological thinking.

4. For a helpful overview of the insights of feminist psychology as they apply to ministry, see Smith (1989), especially pp. 22–42. Ice (1987) has also drawn on the insights of feminist psychology in her study of the worldviews of clergy women.

5. In his helpful book *Frameworks*, Walrath (1987) illustrates in some detail the impact of generational differences on the construction of reality and considers the implications for church leadership.

6. Several of these dimensions of congregational differences are illustrated in a study of congregations in the Hartford, Connecticut, area. My colleagues and I (Roozen, McKinney, and Carroll 1984) used orientations to mission to distinguish congregations. Based on whether their primary emphasis was on this-worldly or otherworldly aspects of Christian life, and whether they emphasized congregational initiative or left action to individual members, we distinguished four orientations. We described some this-worldly congregations as primarily *activist* and others as primarily *civic* in their mission orientations. The mission orientations of other-worldly congregations were either primarily *evangelistic* or the congregations viewed their mission in terms of being a *sanctu-*

ary apart from the world. These orientations reflect different styles of being the church, both in the congregations' internal functioning and in their relation to their social context. We also tried to account for these differences in terms of such things as history, size, location, ethnicity, and leadership.

7. In his important and highly original book *Congregation* (1987), Hopewell not only analyzes the various elements of congregational narrative but also provides helpful guides for those wishing to undertake such an analysis of their own congregation. See also *The Handbook for Congregational Studies* (Carroll, Dudley, and McKinney 1986) for additional ways of studying congregational identity and culture.

8. An exceptionally helpful understanding of tradition and traditioning is found in Schreiter's *Constructing Local Theologies* (1985).

9. See, for example, Meeks (1983) and Gager (1975), who use sociological and anthropological theory to interpret the experiences of various New Testament communities. Dudley and Hilgert (1987) have been quite explicit in trying to draw parallels between the social experiences of the New Testament communities and those of contemporary congregations.

10. For a helpful discussion of the use of church history in congregational decision-making, see Jane Dempsey Douglass (1988).

11. For a guide to understanding and analyzing congregational settings, see the chapter entitled "Context" in Carroll, Dudley, and McKinney (1986). See also Carroll (1988).

Chapter 8
Representing the Sacred and Reflective Leadership

1. A provocative treatment of this perspective is expressed in the book *Resident Aliens*, by Hauerwas and Willimon (1989). While I believe that Hauerwas and Willimon overstate their case for the church's "otherness," I resonate with their call for the church, as embodied especially in congregations, to accept its role as the symbolic presence in the world of our hope in the coming kingdom of God.

2. See Holifield (1983, 304ff.) for a discussion of the struggle of writers on pastoral theology such as Carroll Wise

and Wayne Oates to resist a purely psychological understanding of counseling and to reclaim a distinctly pastoral and religious dimension to the process. Oates was especially sensitive to the symbolic role of the pastor and the institutional setting of *pastoral* counseling in the church, with all that this setting symbolizes.

3. Reed (1978) has explored this experience, especially linked to the worship of the church, in his book *The Dynamics of Religion*. The experience, which he calls "regression to extra-dependence" takes both healthy and unhealthy forms. See also Holmes (1978, 86ff.) for a discussion of priests and the phenomenon of projection.

4. A recent book, *The Soul of the Salesman* (Oakes 1990), analyzes the moral ethos of personal sales and points to the moral contradictions and paradoxes that face those involved in personal sales.

5. There are, of course, widely different conceptions of God—from stern judge and lawgiver to loving parent. How do different conceptions of God affect expectations that people bring to relationships with clergy as sacramental persons? How does clergy behavior affect people's conceptions of God? These are important and interesting questions that are beyond my capacity to explore here. They probably, however, have significant implications for clergy authority and functioning.

6. I have borrowed this phrase from Judy Collins, who used it in an interview with Bill Moyers on PBS to describe the bond between singer and audience that she experienced when singing "Amazing Grace."

7. The sociologist Parsons (1949) has made this distinction between role and motivation regarding professionals in general. Professionals are not, for example, necessarily more altruistic than businesspersons. Rather, Parsons noted, it is the institutional setting of the professional role that differs from that of the businessperson's. The professional's *role* carries with it the expectation that the professional will subordinate self-interest to the client's or community's interest, and various codes of professional ethics try to spell out what this means. The same role expectations do not necessarily succeed for the businessperson. They allow for greater expression of self-interest. Parsons' point is that role expectations and personal

motivations are not the same. The businessperson may, in fact, be more altruistically motivated, on a personal level, than the professional. This distinction between the normative obligations of the role and the motivation and character of the professional is in a peculiar way akin to the Donatist controversy early in the Church's history. The Donatists held that the effectiveness of the priest depended upon the priest's moral disposition. The church fathers, however, followed Augustine and argued instead for an indelible priestly character, given at ordination, that cannot be erased by the priest's inner disposition. This early distinction has at least a surface resemblance to Parsons' distinction between professional role expectations and the professional's inner motives. The difference is that Parsons argues in terms of a sociologically defined role, whereas Augustine argued for an ontologically given, indelible character.

8. H. Richard Niebuhr (1956, 63ff.) identified four elements of the call: (1) the call to be a Christian, the call to discipleship that comes to all Christians; (2) the secret call by which one feels an inner compulsion to enter the ordained ministry; (3) the providential call, evidence that one has the intellectual, moral, physical, and psychological gifts needed for ordained ministry; and (4) the ecclesiastical call, the invitation to serve of a particular church body.

WORKS CITED

Alston, Wallace M., Jr.
    1970   "The Minister as Theologian." Unpublished
            lecture presented at the Duke Divinity School
            Seminars, Columbia, S.C.

Ammerman, Nancy T.
    1987   *Bible Believers.* New Brunswick, N.J.: Rutgers
            University Press.

Argyris, Chris, and Donald A. Schön
    1974   *Theory in Practice.* San Francisco: Jossey-Bass.

Barber, Bernard
    1983   *The Logic and Limits of Trust.* New Brunswick,
            N.J.: Rutgers University Press.

Barth, Karl
    1962   *Church Dogmatics.* Vol. IV, 4. 2. Tr. G. W.
            Bromiley. Edinburgh: T. and T. Clark.

Berger, Peter L.
    1967   *The Sacred Canopy.* Garden City, N.Y.:
            Doubleday & Co.

Berger, Peter L., and Thomas Luckmann
    1966   *The Social Construction of Reality.* Garden City,
            N.Y.: Doubleday & Co.

Bellah, Robert, et al.
    1985   *Habits of the Heart.* Berkeley, Calif.: University
            of California Press.

Bibbey, Reginald W.
    1987   *Fragmented Gods.* Toronto: Irwin.

Bledstein, Burton J.
    1976   *The Culture of Professionalism.* New York: W. W.
            Norton & Co.

Blizzard, Samuel W.
    1956   "The Minister's Dilemma," *The Christian Century*
            25: 508–509.

    1985   *The Protestant Parish Minister: A Behavioral
            Science Interpretation.* Society for the Scientific
            Study of Religion Monograph Series, no. 5.
            Storrs, Conn.: Society for the Scientific Study of
            Religion.

Bonhoeffer, Dietrich
    1955   *Ethics.* Ed. Eberhard Bethge. New York:
            Macmillan Co.

Brooms, Ivan
    1988   "The Whole Christ: A Recovery of Social
            Concern as It Relates to the Gospel." D.Min.
            project, Hartford Seminary.

Browning, Don S.
    1983   "Integrating the Approaches: A Practical
            Theology." In *Building Effective Ministry,* ed.
            Carl S. Dudley, 220–237. San Francisco: Harper
            & Row.

Broyard, Anatole
    1990   "Doctor, Talk to Me." *The New York Times
            Magazine,* (August 26):32–36.

Calhoun, Daniel H.
    1965   *Professional Lives in America.* Cambridge, Mass.:
            Harvard University Press.

Carroll, Jackson W.
    1986   *Ministry as Reflective Practice.* Washington, D.C.:
            The Alban Institute.

1981   "Some Issues in Clergy Authority." *Review of Religious Research* 23:99–117.

1988   "The Congregation as Chameleon: How the Past Interprets the Present." In *Congregations: Their Power to Form and Transform*, ed. C. Ellis Nelson, 43–69. Atlanta: John Knox Press.

Carroll, Jackson W., Carl S. Dudley, and William McKinney, eds.

1986   *Handbook for Congregational Studies.* Nashville: Abingdon Press.

Cooke, Bernard

1975   *Ministry to Word and Sacrament.* Philadelphia: Fortress Press.

Crabtree, Davida Foy

1988   "Empowering the Ministry of the Laity in Workplace, Home and Community: A Programatic and Systemic Approach in the Local Church." D.Min. project, Hartford Seminary.

1989   *The Empowering Church.* Washington, D.C.: The Alban Institute.

Craddock, Fred

1979   *As One Without Authority.* Nashville: Abingdon Press.

Dewey, John

1933   *How We Think.* Chicago: Henry Regnery.

Dillard, Annie

1977   *Holy the Firm.* New York: Harper & Row.

Douglass, H. Paul

1926   *The Springfield Survey.* New York: George H. Doran.

Douglass, H. Paul, and Edmund deS. Brunner

1935   *The Protestant Church as a Social Institution.* New York: Russell & Russell.

Douglass, Jane Dempsey

1988   "A Study of the Congregation in History." In *Beyond Clericalism: The Congregation as a Focus for Theological Education,* ed. Joseph C. Hough, Jr., and Barbara G. Wheeler, 63–75. Atlanta: Scholars Press.

Dozier, Verna
    1982   *The Authority of the Laity.* Washington, D.C.: The Alban Institute.

Dudley, Carl S.
    1987   "Process." Unpublished lecture, Unitarian Universalist Association Congregational Studies Institute, Cambridge, Mass., August.

Dudley, Carl S., and Earle Hilgert
    1987   *New Testament Tensions and the Contemporary Church.* Philadelphia: Fortress Press.

Dudley, Carl S., Jackson W. Carroll, and James P. Wind
    1991   *Carriers of Faith: Lessons from Congregational Studies.* Louisville, Ky.: Westminster/John Knox Press.

Dulles, Avery, S. J.
    1978   *Models of the Church.* Garden City, N.Y.: Doubleday & Co.

Durkheim, Emile
    1915   *The Elementary Forms of Religious Life.* Tr. Joseph W. Swain. London: George Allen & Unwin.

Eliade, Mircea
    1959   *The Sacred and the Profane.* New York: Harper & Row.

Ellul, Jacques
    1964   *The Technological Society.* New York: Random House.

Erikson, Erik H.
    1969   *Gandhi's Truth.* New York: W. W. Norton & Co.

Farley, Edward
    1983   *Theologia.* Philadelphia: Fortress Press.

Festinger, Leon
    1957   *A Theory of Cognitive Dissonance.* Palo Alto, Calif.: Stanford University Press.

Fletcher, John C.
1975   *Religious Authenticity in the Clergy.* Washington,
       D.C.: The Alban Institute.

Freud, Sigmund
1961   *Civilization and Its Discontents.* Tr. James
       Strachey. New York: W. W. Norton & Co.

Gager, John G.
1975   *Kingdom and Community.* Englewood Cliffs, N.J.:
       Prentice-Hall.

Gillespie, Thomas W.
1978   "The Laity in Biblical Perspective." In *The New
       Laity,* ed. Ralph D. Bucy, 13–33. Waco, Tex.:
       Word, 1978.

Greene, Graham
1946   *The Power and the Glory.* New York: Viking
       Books.

Gustafson, James M.
1963   "The Clergy in the United States." *Daedalus* 92
       (Fall):724–744.

1982   "Professions as Callings." *The Social Service
       Review* 56:501–515.

Hadden, Jeffrey K.
1969   *The Gathering Storm in the Churches.* Garden
       City, N.Y.: Doubleday & Co.

Hahn, Celia A.
1985   *Lay Voices in an Open Church.* Washington, D.C.:
       The Alban Institute.

Harlan, David
1980   *The Clergy and the Great Awakening in New
       England.* Ann Arbor, Mich.: UMI Research Press.

Harrison, Paul M.
1959   *Authority and Power in the Free Church Tradition.*
       Princeton, N.J.: Princeton University Press.

Hauerwas, Stanley, and William H. Willimon
1989   *Resident Aliens.* Nashville: Abingdon Press.

Hoge, Dean R.
	1976	*Division in the Protestant House.* Philadelphia: Westminster Press.

Hoge, Dean R., Jackson W. Carroll, and Francis K. Scheets
	1989	*Patterns of Parish Leadership.* Kansas City, Mo.: Sheed & Ward.

Holifield, E. Brooks
	1983	*A History of Pastoral Care in America.* Nashville: Abingdon Press.

Hollar, Larry
	1988	"Haiti: A People's Struggle for Hope." Bread for the World Background Paper No. 107 (September).

Holmes, Urban
	1971	*The Future Shape of Ministry.* New York: Seabury Press.

	1978	*The Priest in Community.* New York: Seabury Press.

Hopewell, James
	1987	*Congregation: Stories and Structures.* Philadelphia: Fortress Press.

Hough, Joseph C., Jr., and John B. Cobb, Jr.
	1985	*Christian Identity and Theological Education.* Atlanta: Scholars Press.

Hughes, Everett C.
	1968	"Professions." *Daedalus* 92:649–668.

Hunter, James D.
	1983	*American Evangelicalism: Conservative Religion and the Quandary of Modernity.* New Brunswick, N.J.: Rutgers University Press.

Ice, Martha L.
	1987	*Clergywomen and Their Worldviews.* New York: Praeger Publishers.

Kelley, Dean M.
	1972	*Why Conservative Churches Are Growing.* San Francisco: Harper & Row.

Kelsey, David H.
1975   *The Uses of Scripture in Recent Theology.*
Philadelphia: Fortress Press.

Keneally, Thomas
1968   *Three Cheers for the Paraclete.* New York: Viking
Books.

King, Luther W.
1981   "An Historical Study of Ministerial Authority in
American Methodism: 1760 to 1940." Ph.D.
diss., Columbia University.

Kirk, Richard J.
1983   "Goodbye and Amen to Father Mulcahy." *Alban
Institute Action Information* 9:7–8.

Klapp, Orrin
1969   *Collective Search for Identity.* New York: Holt,
Rinehart & Winston.

Kleinman, Sherryl
1984   *Equals Before God: Seminarians as Humanistic
Professionals.* Chicago: University of Chicago
Press.

Kratt, Mary
1979   *Marney.* Charlotte, N.C.: Myers Park Baptist
Church.

Kurfiss, Joanne G.
1988   *Critical Thinking: Theory, Research, Practice, and
Possibilities.* ASHE-ERIC Higher Education
Report No. 2. Washington, D.C.: Association for
the Study of Higher Education.

Larson, Magali S.
1977   *The Rise of Professionalism: A Sociological
Analysis.* Berkeley, Calif.: University of
California Press.

Leege, David C.
1986   "Parish Life Among the Leaders." *Notre Dame
Study of Parish Life* 9.

Long, Thomas
1985   "Moses, Aaron, and Practical Theology."
Theology Today 42:1.

Luckmann, Thomas
    1967   *The Invisible Religion.* New York: Macmillan Co.

Luker, Kristin
    1984   *Abortion and the Politics of Motherhood.* Berkeley,
            Calif.: University of California Press.

Lukes, Steven
    1978   "Power and Authority." In *A History of
            Sociological Analysis,* eds. Robert Nisbet and
            Thomas Bottomore, 633–676. New York: Basic
            Books.

Lutheran Church in America
    1984   *God's People in Ministry.* Philadelphia: Division
            for Professional Leadership.

Lyotard, Jean-François
    1984   *The Post-Modern Condition.* Tr. Geoff Bennington
            and Brian Massumi. Minneapolis: University of
            Minnesota Press.

MacIntyre, Alasdair
    1981   *After Virtue.* Notre Dame, Ind.: University of
            Notre Dame Press.

Marty, Martin
    1970   *Righteous Empire: The Protestant Experience in
            America.* New York: Dial Press.

Matthews, Dale A., Anthony L. Suchman, and William T.
Branch, Jr.
    n.d.   "Making Connexions." Unpublished paper,
            University of Connecticut Health Center.

McClelland, David C.
    1975   *Power: The Inner Experience.* New York: Irvington
            Publishers.

McKinney, William, David A. Roozen, and Jackson W. Carroll
    1983   *Religion's Public Presence.* Washington, D.C.: The
            Alban Institute.

Mead, Loren B.
    1976   "Authority and Religious Authority." *Alban
            Institute Action Information* (December).

Mead, Sidney
    1956   "The Rise of the Evangelical Conception of Ministry in America (1607–1850)." In *The Ministry in Historical Perspectives*, eds. H. Richard Niebuhr and Daniel Day Williams, 207–249. New York: Harper & Row.

Meeks, Wayne A.
    1983   *The First Urban Christians: The Social World of the Apostle Paul*. New Haven, Conn.: Yale University Press.

Moberg, David
    1972   *The Great Reversal: Evangelism versus Social Concern*. Philadelphia: J. B. Lippincott Co.

Mock, Alan K., James D. Davidson, and C. Lincoln Johnson
    1991   "Threading the Needle: Faith and Works in Affluent Churches." In *Carriers of Faith: Lessons from Congregational Studies*, eds. Carl S. Dudley, Jackson W. Carroll, and James P. Wind, 86–102. Louisville, Ky.: Westminster/John Knox Press.

Niebuhr, H. Richard
    1941   *The Meaning of Revelation*. New York: Macmillan Co.

    1956   *The Purpose of the Church and Its Ministry*. New York: Harper & Row.

Nisbet, Robert
    1966   *The Sociological Tradition*. New York: Basic Books.

O'Dea, Thomas
    1966   *The Sociology of Religion*. Englewood Cliffs, N.J.: Prentice-Hall.

Oakes, Guy
    1990   *The Soul of The Salesman*. Atlantic Highlands, N.J.: Humanities Press International.

Palmer, Parker J.
    1990   *To Know as We Are Known: A Spirituality of Education*. San Francisco: Harper & Row.

Parsons, Talcott
    1937/1949   *The Structure of Social Action.* New York:
          The Free Press.
    1949   *Essays in Sociological Theory: Pure and Applied.*
          New York: The Free Press.

Polanyi, Michael
    1958   *Personal Knowledge.* Chicago: University of
          Chicago Press.

Quinley, Harold
    1974   *The Prophetic Clergy.* New York: John Wiley &
          Sons.

Reed, Bruce
    1978   *The Dynamics of Religion.* London: Darton,
          Longman & Todd.

Rieff, Philip
    1966   *The Triumph of the Therapeutic.* New York:
          Harper & Row.

Roof, Wade Clark, and William McKinney
    1987   *American Mainline Religion.* New Brunswick,
          N.J.: Rutgers University Press.

Roozen, David A., William McKinney, and Jackson W. Carroll
    1984   *Varieties of Religious Presence.* New York: Pilgrim
          Press.

Russell, Anthony
    1980   *The Clerical Profession.* London: SPCK.

Russell, Letty
    1979   *The Future of Partnership.* Philadelphia:
          Westminster Press.
    1987   *Household of Freedom.* Philadelphia: Westminster
          Press.

Sanchez, José
    1972   *Anticlericalism: A Brief History.* Notre Dame,
          Ind.: Notre Dame Press.

Sartre, Jean-Paul
    1956   *Being and Nothingness.* Tr. Hazel Barnes. New
          York: Philosophical Library.

Schillebeeckx, Edward
    1981   *Ministry.* New York: Crossroad.
    1985   *The Church with a Human Face.* New York: Crossroad.

Schmotter, James W.
    1973   "Provincial Professionalism: The New England Ministry, 1692–1745." Ph.D. diss., Northwestern University.

Schön, Donald A.
    1983   *The Reflective Practitioner.* New York: Basic Books.
    1987   *Educating the Reflective Practitioner.* San Francisco: Jossey-Bass.

Schreiter, Robert
    1985   *Constructing Local Theologies.* Maryknoll, N.Y.: Orbis Books.

Schuller, David S., Milo L. Brekke, and Merton P. Strommen
    1975   *Readiness for Ministry,* vol 1. Vandalia, Ohio: Association of Theological Schools.
    1980   *Ministry in America.* San Francisco: Harper & Row.

Schweizer, Eduard
    1961   *Church Order in the New Testament.* London: SCM Press.

Scott, Donald M.
    1978   *From Office to Profession.* Philadelphia: University of Pennsylvania Press.

Selznick, Philip
    1957   *Leadership in Administration.* New York: Harper & Row.

Sennett, Richard
    1980   *Authority.* New York: Alfred A. Knopf.

Shütz, John
    1975   *Paul and the Anatomy of Apostolic Authority.* Cambridge: Cambridge University Press.

Smith, Christine M.
     1989   *Weaving the Sermon: Preaching in a Feminist*
               Perspective. Louisville, Ky.: Westminster/John
               Knox Press.

Smith, H. Shelton, Robert Handy, and Lefferts A. Loetcher
     1960   *American Christianity.* New York: Charles
               Scribner's Sons.

Starr, Paul
     1982   *The Social Transformation of American Medicine.*
               New York: Basic Books.

Stout, Harry S.
     1986   *The New England Soul.* New York: Oxford
               University Press.

     1987   "Soundings from New England: Mainline
               Protestants Today." *The Reformed Journal*
               37:7–12.

Suchman, Anthony L., and Dale A. Matthews
     1988   "What Makes the Patient-Doctor Relationship
               Therapeutic? Exploring the Connexional
               Dimension of Medical Care." *Annals of Internal*
               Medicine 108:125–130.

Sweet, Leonard I.
     1982   "Not All Cats Are Gray: Beyond Liberalism's
               Uncertain Faith." *The Christian Century* (June
               23–30):721–725.

Vallier, Ivan
     1968   "Religious Specialists: Sociological Study." In
               International Encyclopedia of the Social Sciences,
               vol. 12, ed. David Sills, 444–453. New York:
               Crowell, Collier, and Macmillan.

Voye, Lillian
     1989   "From Institutional Catholicism to 'Christian
               Inspiration'." Unpublished paper.

Wach, Joachim
     1944   *Sociology of Religion.* Chicago: University of
               Chicago Press.

Walrath, Douglas A.
    1987   *Frameworks, Patterns for Living and Believing
            Today.* New York: Pilgrim Press.

Weber, Max
    1958a   *The Protestant Ethic and the Spirit of Capitalism.*
            Tr. Talcott Parsons. New York: Charles
            Scribner's Sons.

    1958b   *From Max Weber: Essays in Sociology.* Tr. and ed.
            H. H. Gerth and C. Wright Mills. New York:
            Oxford University Press.

    1963   *The Sociology of Religion.* Tr. Ephraim Fischoff.
            Boston: Beacon Press.

    1968   *Economy and Society.* Eds. Guenther Roth and
            Claus Wittich. New York: Bedminster Press.

Whitehead, James D. and Evelyn Eaton Whitehead
    1981   *Method in Ministry: Theological Reflection and
            Christian Ministry.* New York: Seabury Press.

Willems, Emilio
    1967   "Validation and Authority in Pentecostal Sects
            of Chile and Brazil." *Journal for the Scientific
            Study of Religion* 4:253–258.

Wood, Charles M.
    1985   *Vision and Discernment.* Atlanta: Scholars Press.

Wood, James R.
    1981   *Leadership in Voluntary Organizations.* New
            Brunswick, N.J.: Rutgers University Press.

World Council of Churches
    1982   *Baptism, Eucharist and Ministry.* Faith and Order
            Paper No. 111. Geneva: World Council of
            Churches.

Yankelovich, Daniel
    1981   *New Rules.* New York: Random House.

Youngs, J. William T.
    1976   *God's Messengers: Religious Leadership in Colonial
            New England, 1700–1750.* Baltimore: Johns
            Hopkins Press.

Index

INDEX